Tales from the
San Francisco Giants Dugout

Nick Peters

Sports Publishing L.L.C.
www.SportsPublishingLLC.com

Director of production: Susan M. Moyer
Project manager: Greg Hickman
Developmental editor: Gabe Rosen
Copy editor: Cynthia L. McNew
Dust jacket design: Christine Mohrbacher

ISBN: 1-58261-686-8

Printed in the United States.

SPORTS PUBLISHING L.L.C.
www.SportsPublishingLLC.com

To the good old days
and the Giants who helped to make them that way.

Acknowledgments

I've been following the club since its move westward, witnessing many of its vignettes as a baseball writer since 1961. I am indebted to fellow journalists like Bob Stevens, Art Rosenbaum, Charles Einstein, Jack McDonald, Curley Grieve, Bucky Walter, Jack Hanley, and Harry Jupiter, who chronicled the Giants during their early days in The City.

I am also appreciative of the storytelling talents of broadcasters Russ Hodges, Lon Simmons, Hank Greenwald, Ron Fairly, Mike Krukow, Duane Kuiper and Jon Miller, and the memories of colleagues Glenn Schwarz, Ron Bergman, Dan McGrath, John Hillyer, Ron Bergman, John Shea and Ray Ratto.

Finally, I am grateful that Mike Mandel and Steve Bitker authored fine oral histories of the Giants. And, of course, I'm thankful for all the players and managers who made 45 years memorable, win or lose.

Contents

In the Beginning, Horace:

The Giants Move from the Polo Grounds to Seals Stadium

No Love Lost

Fans attending the Giants' final home game at the Polo Grounds, Sept. 27, 1957, were sad to see the team depart for San Francisco, but they didn't mind being rid of owner Horace Stoneham. The following chant was repeated several times during the nostalgic afternoon:

> "We want Stoneham.
> "We want Stoneham.
> "We want Stoneham...
> "With a rope around his neck."

How About The Kids?

When Horace Stoneham finally received permission from the board of directors to move the Giants, the announcement was greeted with bitterness and anger by longtime fans. But their numbers obviously were dwindling.

A reporter asked Stoneham, "How about all the kids who won't be able to come to the Polo Grounds?" His curt reply: "I don't know about the kids, but I haven't seen many of their fathers lately."

The Great Arrival

It was a perfect day at Seals Stadium, April 15,1958, when the Giants and the Dodgers introduced major-league baseball to the West Coast before an overflow crowd of 23,448. For the partisans, it was storybook stuff.

The Giants were staking their future on a new look, starting three rookies in the opening lineup: first baseman Orlando Cepeda, third baseman Jim Davenport, and right fielder Willie Kirkland. They didn't disappoint.

Cepeda hit a 370-foot homer to right center, Davenport singled twice, and Kirkland singled and was robbed of extra bases by Gino Cimoli, who became the answer to the trivia question: Who was the first batter in that historic Opening Day?

The veterans sparkled, too. Ruben Gomez went the distance in an 8-0 victory, and Darryl Spencer hit the first home run (off Don Drysdale). Willie Mays contributed a two-run single, lost his cap chasing down a fly in center field, and summed up: "It's like a World Series."

"We've inherited some real fans," manager Bill Rigney said. "They knew when to cheer. They gave Cimoli a big hand for his catch, and I liked that. And imagine having three rookies on the field all acting as if they'd been around for years."

It Took Some Time

Old habits are hard to break. Shortly after the final out, special late afternoon editions of San Francisco newspapers proclaimed the great victory, and a popular downtown vendor at Union Square barked: "New York Giants win opener!"

He wasn't alone, of course. Giants announcer Russ Hodges frequently used "New York" while describing the team over the airwaves in the early days, promptly correcting himself so as not to offend provincial San Franciscans.

Nobody seemed to mind. The city was in a state of euphoria over the Giants. Former NL batting champion Lefty O'Doul, then a prominent S.F. tavern owner, declared after the 8-0 triumph: "Everyone in this town is unconscious."

Walter "The Great" Mails, a former major-league pitcher serving as the Giants' new promotional director, summed up: "Any new show that comes here with a New York trademark is a guaranteed success. Our people expect the best from New York."

The Comeback Kids

Giants fans took to their new team in 1958 because of a promising crop of rookies and the club's comeback character, which was best exemplified on the afternoon of May 5, 1958, at Seals Stadium.

The Pittsburgh Pirates entered the bottom of the ninth with a whopping 11-1 lead, and several spectators already were headed home. What they missed was one of the greatest rallies in franchise history.

Manager Bill Rigney, his roster depleted, kept coming up with the right moves and pinch hitters Jim King, Johnny Antonelli, and Bob Speake delivered doubles in a nine-run rally that made it 11-10. (Ray Jablonski's three-run homer was the big blow.)

With the bases loaded and two outs, the storybook ending fizzled. Pinch hitter Don Taussig, batting for Antonelli, popped out to second baseman Bill Mazeroski in a tight finish that typified the club's early years in San Francisco.

A Close Shave

Valmy Thomas was minding his business while shaving in the clubhouse shower room at Connie Mack Stadium, July 24, 1958, during a trip to Philadelphia. Suddenly, an electrical storm produced a bolt of lighting that shocked the Giants' catcher.

It shot through a window, bounced off the metal whirlpool tub and struck the pipes under the washbasin Thomas was using. Sparks lighted up the room, but Thomas calmly continued to shave following a brief pause.

"It never strikes twice in the same place," Thomas explained with a smile.

A Better Pitcher Than Driver

Sam Jones was such a bad driver that nobody wanted to ride with him. But Sad Sam hated to fly, so when he wanted to drive his family from Chicago to Detroit during the 1959 All-Star break, catcher Hobie Landrith agreed to go with him—on one condition.

"I told Sam that if he gave me the keys to the car and let me drive all the way, I'd go with him," Landrith recalled. "So he has his wife and two children in the car, and we leave right after the ballgame and drive all night.

"He reaches for the cigarette lighter, and instead of pulling it out straight, he pulls it out at an angle, jerks it and shorts out the entire electrical system. I'm going down the highway at 70 mph, and suddenly there's no lights.

"So Sam finds his flashlight and we drive for two or three hours with Sam holding his flashlight out the back window every time there was a car approaching from the rear. Needless to say, once we got to Detroit, I flew back."

Like Going to Disneyland

After the Giants won two out of three from the Dodgers at Seals Stadium on their opening West Coast series, there was more commotion when the two clubs switched to the L.A. Coliseum for a three-game weekend set.

The Dodgers, playing before a new major-league-record crowd of 78,672, satisfied the huge throng with a 6-5 victory, but the Giants roared back to win the next two games 11-4 and 12-2 behind Ruben Gomez and Ramon Monzant.

"Disneyland," Hank Sauer joyously declared after the aging slugger walloped three home runs in the series, lofting towering flies over the 40-foot left field screen, 250 feet from home plate down the line

"If you hit the ball in the air to left, it was a home run. Yet some balls that were hit hard hit the top of the screen and came back. The Dodgers tried to make a deal for me so I could play every day in that ballpark, but Horace Stoneham wouldn't let me go."

Davvy's Day

Among the Giants' bounty of talented rookies in 1958, Orlando Cepeda received the most recognition, earning Rookie of the Year honors. But third baseman Jim Davenport also sparkled, fielding brilliantly.

On Sept. 12, it was all Davenport in a 5-2, 19-2 doubleheader sweep of the host Philadelphia Phillies. In fact, few rookies have enjoyed a better day: seven hits in 10 at-bats, including a home run in each game, seven runs, and four RBI.

A Premature Celebration

The Giants thought they had the 1959 pennant won on Sept. 17, when Willie Mays's three-run homer powered a 13-6 rout of the Milwaukee Braves at Seals Stadium. The convincing victory gave the Giants a two-game lead over the Braves and the Dodgers with eight games remaining.

"This was for the pennant!" usually conservative manager Bill Rigney declared following the impressive win, one in which the Giants' balanced 14-hit attack overcame Eddie Mathews's two homers and six RBI. The Giants knocked Warren Spahn from the game before an out was registered in the three-run first inning.

Spahn was going for his 20th victory, but came unglued in the opening inning on singles by Mays and Orlando Cepeda. Willie Mays finished with four hits and five RBI; leadoff hitter Eddie Bressoud added four runs and three hits, including a homer, and Jim Davenport homered and had four RBI.

"Two up with eight to go, only the total disintegration of this Rigney-steered machine can keep it from bringing to the city by the Golden Gate its first professional team championship in all its multi-titled history," Bob Steven wrote in the *San Francisco Chronicle*.

But the Giants did indeed disintegrate. A three-game weekend sweep by the Dodgers at Seals Stadium gave them a half-game edge over the Braves, knocking the Giants to third. And that's how the race finished one week later, because the Giants dropped four out of five at Chicago and St. Louis.

The '60s
A Decade of Superstars and Seconds:

Mays, McCovey and Marichal ... Mmmmmm, Good

A Friendly Wager

When Whitey Ford fired a called third strike past Mays to end the first inning of the 1961 All-Star Game at Candlestick Park, center fielder Mickey Mantle showed unusual enthusiasm over the achievement of his New York Yankees teammate.

The explanation surfaced years later when Mantle told of an invitation extended by Giants owner Horace Stoneham to the two Yankees the day before the game. They played golf and had lunch at the famed Olympic Club and Mantle recalled:

"Horace said to Whitey, 'If you get Willie out, I'll sign for everything.' But if Willie got a hit, we'd have to pay for everything. Well, we wound up with a bill for over $400 that day.

"So, when Whitey struck out Mays, I came runnin' in from center field, jumpin' in the air like we'd just won the World Series. Nobody could figure it out—except Horace Stoneham."

Secret Weapon

Willie Mays (49 homers) and Jack Sanford (24 wins) received the bulk of the credit for the 1962 pennant, but the Giants' secret weapon down the stretch was outfielder Felipe Alou, who enjoyed his finest S.F. season with a .316 average, 25 home runs and 98 RBI.

Alou made the All-Star team and took off afterward to power several key victories. In a three-game August sweep of the Dodgers at Candlestick, for instance, he was eight for 12 with seven runs scored. Then his two-run, ninth-inning homer off Jim Brosnan edged the Cincinnati Reds 6-4, Sept. 2.

In a series with the Chicago Cubs, Felipe drilled nine straight hits and won two games with home runs, Sept. 7-9. His two-run homer off Tom Sturdivant defeated the Pittsburgh Pirates 3-2, Sept. 11. He finished the season batting .342 with 16 RBI against the Dodgers and batted .438 (seven for 16) in the World Series.

"Felipe comes closest to Willie Mays at being great," manager Alvin Dark declared. "Felipe is the second best outfielder in the league. After Mays, he's as good as anybody."

Exactly 40 years after his greatest season with the Giants, the 67-year-old Alou was named as the club's manager for 2003, and his 7-0 start was the best in S.F. history.

A Winning Hand

The suddenly inept Dodgers seemed doomed when the best-of-three playoff series opened Oct. 1 at Candlestick Park. After blowing a four-game lead with seven to go, they entered the playoffs without a run in 21 consecutive innings and were facing left-hander Billy Pierce, who hadn't lost at home all season.

Sure enough, Pierce extended their scoreless streak to 30 innings with a three-hitter, and the incomparable Mays homered twice in an 8-0 romp before 32,660. Pierce thereby improved to 12-0 at Candlestick, Willie Mays grabbed the major-league lead with 49 home runs, and the Giants had a leg up in the series.

Sandy Koufax, winless since July 12 after injuring his index finger, fell behind quickly when Felipe Alou lined a two-out double into the left field corner and Mays followed with a homer to right-center in the first inning. He was lifted in the second, shortly after Jim Davenport homered. Mays and Orlando Cepeda hit back-to-back homers in the sixth.

"This game gave me the greatest satisfaction of my life," said Pierce, who was 16-6 that season. It also made the Giants the favorites to reach the World Series. The New York Yankees apparently thought so, too, checking into a San Francisco hotel before the playoffs began.

The Dodgers' demise—11 losses in 14 games—baffled the nation's press, and the great Red Smith was compelled to write:

"It was the sorriest collapse since the Tower of Babel, the most abject surrender since Appomattox Court House. If these guys had been at Valley Forge, we'd still be singing 'God Save the Queen.'"

"These People Are Crazy"

When the Giants headed home following their pennant clincher in Los Angeles, they had no idea how many fans wanted to join the celebration. They were on their team bus heading for the airport, when announcer Russ Hodges began singing, a la Tony Bennett: "We're coming home to you, San Francisco...with a pennant in the bag."

There was jubilation on the short flight home, but nothing compared to what was going on in the streets of San Francisco. Fans, overcome with joy, headed for the airport to form a huge reception committee, and there were so many of them, that landing in Oakland was a consideration.

A crowd estimated at 100,000 crashed through police lines and stormed the runway. As wary players climbed off the charter flight and onto the team bus, they were mobbed by fans, many pounding the bus.

"These people are crazy!" Jim Davenport declared after an exuberant fan shattered a window, causing him to head for the aisle. For Willie Mays's safety, it was suggested that lookalike reserve Carl Boles be thrust out the door as a sacrificial lamb.

Added Willie McCovey: "They couldn't control the crowd. By the time we got off the plane and onto the bus, people started rocking the bus. I thought they were going to turn it over. It was pretty scary."

Hitching A Ride

When the Giants' bus finally reached Candlestick Park, the 1962 pennant winners had another dilemma before being thrown to the Yankees. Willie Mays caught one of the few available taxis, but many of his teammates had to hitch rides home on the nearby Bayshore Freeway.

"We were walking along the highway, and a lady pulled up in a station wagon with curlers in her hair," playoff hero Billy Pierce recalled. "She didn't know who we were, and asked, 'Are you fellows ballplayers?'

"She took us to San Mateo and kept trying to hide her hair while she was driving. That's the only time I ever hitched a ride in my life."

Willie McCovey and Orlando Cepeda, neighbors in the city's Sunset District, did likewise and were picked up by a fan who couldn't believe his eyes.

"He thought he was hallucinating," McCovey said. "He told us he would take us anywhere we wanted to go. And then when we finally got home, all of our neighbors were out in front of our houses to greet us. We didn't get to bed until early in the morning, and we had to get up to play in the World Series."

Alou! Alou! Alou!

The Giants made major-league history on Sept. 15, 1963, at Forbes Field when the three Alou brothers—Felipe, Mateo and Jesus—comprised the outfield in the eighth and ninth innings of a 13-5 victory over the Pittsburgh Pirates. Mateo was in left, Felipe in center, and Jesus in right.

It marked the first time ever that three siblings patrolled the same outfield. What isn't commonly known, however, is that on Sept. 10 at the Polo Grounds they established another first by batting in succession during an inning. Pinch hitter Jesus led off with a grounder to short, Mateo struck out as a pinch hitter, and Felipe hit an inning-ending grounder.

The Alous were in the same outfield one last time, Sept. 22, in the final three innings of a 13-3 victory over the New York Mets at Candlestick Park. However, they frequently did it in the Dominican Republic Winter League. Felipe (Braves) and Mateo (Pirates) soon were traded to teams for which they blossomed as hitters.

Just Say No

When Ron Hunt was the Giants' second baseman, his forte was being struck by pitches. In fact, he crowded the plate so much that he wore a thick rubber girdle around his waist for added protection.

One day, when teammate Bobby Bonds noticed a huge black bruise on Hunt's body, he quipped: "Ron, believe me, there's no advantage in turning my color."

Hunt, who set a major-league record by being a target of pitches 243 times, was proud of his specialty, boasting: "Some people give their bodies to science; I gave mine to baseball."

The June Swoon

The term "June Swoon" is a misnomer, but it has stuck with the Giants because some midsummer collapses during their early days in San Francisco ultimately cost them dearly at season's end.

Actually, the club hasn't had that many poor Junes, though there have been exceptions. The notion began in 1958, when the club went 10-17 in June and dropped out of the lead. Ditto in 1960, when an 11-16 June cost them four and one-half games in the standings. In 1968, a 14-17 June greased a seven-game slide.

And, come to think of it, June has been their worst month in the first 45 years of their West Coast existence, a composite 618-625 record (.497) representing their lone losing month.

"I wish June and swoon didn't rhyme," witty catcher Bob Brenly once said. "If they didn't, no one would ever have heard the phrase. Instead, I have to hear it every year."

He Had Horace's Ear

When Bill Rigney was fired with a winning record (33-25) in 1960, he was succeeded by Tom "Clancy" Sheehan, a long-time confidante and scout who sat in owner Horace Stoneham's box. His short-lived reign produced a 46-50 record, a fifth-place finish, and a lot of laughs, because he was a ponderous man clearly overwhelmed by the job.

Once, in a hoarse, booming voice, Sheehan bemoaned the fact that he couldn't improve the club's play and bellowed: "Jesus Christ, you guys looked a lot better up there than you do down here!"

Seldom-used reliever Joe Shipley had the size and the ability to imitate the burly manager and, like most Giants, didn't respect Rig's replacement. At Milwaukee that season, Shipley turned the dislike for Sheehan into comic relief.

Sheehan went to the mound to make a pitching change and motioned to the bullpen, where Shipley and Bud Byerly were warming. Well, signals got crossed, and Shipley was in a golf cart heading for the infield.

"I get there," Shipley recalled, "and Tom says to me, 'Jesus Christ, what are you doing here? I want the other guy. Go back and tell Bud to come in.' So I get in the golf cart, they're taking me back to the bullpen, and everybody starts applauding."

Where's My Pitcher?

During a game in Milwaukee, Sept. 7, Jack Sanford was being roughed up by the Braves, and Sheehan elected to make a pitching change. The burly manager stepped out of the dugout and headed for the pitcher's mound.

"He chugs along with his head down, and Sanford knows he's going out of the game," Stu Miller recalled. "As soon as he sees Santa take that first step, he just shoots by him to the dugout.

"By the time Santa gets out to the mound, he looks around and says, 'Where the hell is my pitcher?' Sanford already was in the dugout. He never saw him go by. We used to laugh at things like that all the time."

Sanford's Streak

Jack Sanford enjoyed one of the finest seasons ever by a San Francisco pitcher when he went 24-7 to lead the staff into the World Series. But it didn't start out that way. After two months, he was a meager 6-6 and temporarily demoted from the rotation by manager Alvin Dark.

But he suddenly learned to control his vaunted temper and opposing batters in a remarkable stretch. Sanford didn't lose from June 14 to Sept. 5, racking up16 consecutive victories and falling three shy of Rube Marquard's major-league-record 19 in a row in 1912.

"I guess I got mad after that," Sanford said of a 5-0 loss to the Cincinnati Reds, June 13, but he certainly wasn't impressed by his feat. "I have no idea who won 19 in a row, and I don't care. A record doesn't mean anything to me."

But the grumpy Sanford softened his stance following the 2-0 shutout of the Pittsburgh Pirates that gave him 16 straight and a 22-6 record, declaring: "Sixteen in a row? This is ridiculous. Nobody wins 16 in a row.

"A good bullpen and the breaks, I guess that's what you need. Sure, you might expect to win five or six in a row, lots of pitchers do, but 16?"

Sanford wasn't the only Giant streaking that day. Felipe Alou entered the game with nine straight hits and grounded out in the first inning before lashing two hits, including a solo homer. That made him 11 for 12.

"Here, Hit It!"

Left-hander Billy O'Dell pitched five years with the Giants, winning 56 games, but he didn't have much success with light-hitting Philadelphia Phillies shortstop Bobby Wine. One day, he decided to alter his strategy, so he told manager Alvin Dark he was merely going to let Wine hit the ball.

"What do you mean—like batting practice?" Dark inquired.

"No," replied O'Dell, "better than that. I'm just going to toss it in there." The next time the Giants played in Philadelphia, there were two on base in a tight game when Wine went to the plate.

"Hey, Bobby, hit this one," O'Dell yelled before virtually lobbing the ball. "I just threw it in, didn't wind up or anything, and he popped it up to the catcher. I did that several times with him, and he never hit one good."

The Longest Day

On May 31, 1964, Gaylord Perry perfected his famous "spitter" in relief against the New York Mets, but that's not all that happened in an arduous Sunday doubleheader at new Shea Stadium. The Mets had won the first two games of the series, and Jim Hickman's three-run homer off Juan Marichal gave them an early lead in the first game.

The Giants, disappointing a crowd of 57,037, rallied for a 5-3 victory and jumped to a 6-1 lead in the second game. But Joe Christopher's three-run homer created a 6-6 tie in the sixth, and the game eventually went into extra innings. Lots of them.

In the 14th, a Giants threat was snuffed when Orlando Cepeda lined into a triple play. By the time Jim Davenport's two-out triple off Galen Cisco and pinch hitter Del Crandall's double paced an 8-6 victory in the 23rd inning, the two teams had played the longest doubleheader in major-league history, with 32 innings consuming 9:52.

The second game also set a record of 7:23 and did not conclude until 11:24 p.m. It included 20 hits by the Mets and 17 by the Giants. Jesus Alou, Tom Haller, Charlie Smith and Christopher each had four hits. Perry worked 10 shutout innings for the win, yielding seven hits, striking out nine and walking one.

"I'm tired, very tired," Willie Mays told a reporter who awakened him the next afternoon. "Playing three games in one day is a lot. When it was over, it was a relief. I don't think I could have played a game today."

Trivia Time

Can you name the Hall of Famers who played for the Giants in the 1960s?

Willie Mays, Juan Marichal, Willie McCovey, Gaylord Perry and Orlando Cepeda are the easy answers.

But there's more.

Give up?

Though their appearances were limited, Warren Spahn and Duke Snider briefly were with the club during the decade. Spahn went 3-4 in 16 games in 1965, and Snider batted .210 in 91 games in 1964.

Knowing the Signs

Tito Fuentes was a rookie shortstop in 1966 when the Giants were at Shea Stadium to play the New York Mets. Ex-Giant Bob Shaw was on the mound, and Fuentes was at the plate in a sacrifice situation.

Shaw went into his stretch, and Fuentes stepped back from the batter's box. This happened three straight times, according to plate umpire Chris Pelekoudas, so a perturbed Shaw came off the mound and yelled at Fuentes.

"What are you doing, Tito?" he asked. "Stay in there and swing!"

"I'm trying to catch the sign from Coach [Charlie] Fox," Fuentes replied.

Shaw snapped back, "He's given you the bunt sign three times already. Now, get back in there!"

McCormick's Redemption

Left-hander Mike McCormick was the staff ace in 1960, when he led the National League with a 2.70 ERA. But he was known as a hard-luck pitcher, going 12-16 in 1959 while losing 14 games in which he yielded three runs or fewer, and 13-16 in 1961 despite a solid 3.20 ERA.

He became expendable when fellow lefties Billy O'Dell and Billy Pierce were successful on the pennant-winning 1962 team and soon was traded to the Baltimore Orioles. After four years in the American League, he returned to the Giants and promptly became their lone Cy Young Award winner, going 22-10 with a 2.85 ERA in 1967. Juan Marichal never did it.

"In 1967, Sandy Koufax had retired," McCormick pointed out. "All the other good pitchers were there, but none of them had great years. Fergie Jenkins and I were the only 20-game winners. Juan struggled and Bob Gibson had a mediocre year. It was just one of those things where all the good pitchers had average years."

That's not the entire story. McCormick, battling for a spot in the rotation, was merely 5-3 after two months while vying with Ray Sadecki for No. 4 honors. But Sadecki was off to a 6-18 start (before winning his last six), and McCormick picked up the slack by going 12-3 with a 2.18 ERA from June 19 to Aug. 27.

"We went to Houston, and somebody had to miss a start," he recalled. "I pitched nine innings and won, so I got another start. I won again, and I kept winning. Because somebody missed a start, they couldn't get me out of the rotation."

Bobby's Booming Bow

When Bobby Bonds was promoted from Triple-A in the summer of 1968, the fleet outfielder was being favorably compared to Willie Mays because of his blend of speed and power. Nothing happened in his debut, June 25, at Dodger Stadium that altered the unfair buildup.

Batting in the No. 7 slot, Bonds went to the plate with the bases loaded in the bottom of the sixth inning and delivered a grand slam home run off reliever John Purdin. The Giants scored six runs that inning and won 9-0 on Ray Sadecki's two-hitter.

"Herman Franks put me in right field and I was excited to be breaking in near my hometown [Riverside]," Bonds said. "The grand slam was my only hit, my first hit. That first hit, you always remember the pitcher and the pitch.

"It certainly was a highlight of my career. I started playing regularly right away. Jesus Alou was there, and they still had Ollie Brown, but I didn't feel that I had to win the job. They called me up to play, and I didn't feel I had to beat out anybody."

Nor was he intimidated by the "next Mays" label. He idolized Mays and even wore No. 24 in the minors, so he was flattered by the comparison. However, he felt it was unrealistic to expect him to be like Mays.

"I always thought of it as a compliment when they would mention his name and mine together," Bonds said. "But you can't carry on for Mays. People like Willie don't come along every day. He's done this thing. You've got to go out and do yours."

The '70s:
The Fall and Rise of the Giants' Empire

Lurie's rescue, McCovey, Blue,
Spark Franchise Comeback

A Daffy Decade

The Giants experienced it all during their most turbulent decade in San Francisco, beginning with great individual accomplishments in 1970 and a division title in 1971 before the franchise fell into disarray with the trading of future Hall of Famers and the eventual collapse of the Horace Stoneham regime.

It started auspiciously in 1970 with Willie McCovey enjoying his last big year (39 homers, 126 RBI); Dick Dietz assembling the best offensive season ever by a S.F. catcher (.300, 22 homers, 107 RBI); Bobby Bonds setting an S.F. record for runs (134); Gaylord Perry winning 23 games; Juan Marichal posting his 200th victory, and Willie Mays notching his 3,000th hit.

"It definitely was up and down," Jim Barr said of the decade. "We were young, and we figured the team would be great for a long time. A couple of years later, all the superstars were gone and we started questioning the stability of the organization. We all worried about the future."

Year of the Fox

The 1971 Giants didn't have a .300 hitter or a 20-game winner, but they won a division title—the first time an NL team had done so without either since 1876. And it was nearly a wire-to-wire triumph for Charlie Fox, who was rewarded with the Manager of the Year distinction.

"Sometimes I still wonder how we won," Fox said many years later. "The Dodgers had a better team, but we played very well together. Giving Chris Speier the shortstop job in spring training was the smartest move I made. Then I put Tito Fuentes at second. Before that, we couldn't turn the double play."

With the sparkling combo leading the way, the Giants bolted to an 18-5 April and expanded their lead to 10 and one-half games in May. The eight-game edge at the start of September dwindled rapidly, however, and it might have cost the club a pennant.

That's because a victory was needed on the final day in San Diego to avoid a tie with the Dodgers. So Juan Marichal started that crucial game instead of the playoff opener, and he beat the Padres 5-1 with the help of a Dave Kingman homer.

But the Pittsburgh Pirates, 3-9 against the Giants during the regular season, rallied after losing Game 1 to Gaylord Perry and won three straight to enter the World Series. Marichal started Game 3 in Pittsburgh and lost 2-1.

"I didn't want to use Juan for the last game of the season," Fox said, "but after we lost on Saturday, I had to use him. Had we clinched earlier, I would have saved Juan for two playoff starts. Had we had a rested Marichal, I think we would have beaten the Pirates."

He Was Inspeiering

When the Giants won their only championship in a span of 25 years in 1971, the catalyst was rookie shortstop Chris Speier of crossbay Alameda. At age 21, he made the leap to major-league stardom following merely one year of minor-league seasoning at Double-A Amarillo.

Taking charge of the infield, Speier formed the best double-play combination in S.F. history with Tito Fuentes and became merely the second rookie shortstop in modern baseball history to play regularly for a championship team. Alvin Dark of the 1948 Boston Braves was the other.

"He's the best shortstop I've ever seen on the Giants," raved pitching coach Larry Jansen, who was with the club since 1947 and observed Dark when Alvin was the shortstop on the New York Giants.

Speier crowned his rookie season by batting .357 against the Pittsburgh Pirates in the playoffs, and one year later, he played in the All-Star Game, was voted the league's premier shortstop and became the first shortstop to lead the Giants in batting since Hall of Famer Travis Jackson in 1926.

Barr's Record Streak

Right-hander Jim Barr was a good pitcher on bad teams during most of his Giants career, winning 64 games in a five-year period, 1973-77, but his greatest achievement was a record-setting performance as a rookie in 1972.

Barr retired 41 consecutive batters without a hit—the equivalent of 13 and two-thirds no-hit innings—over two games against Pittsburgh and St. Louis. The previous record was 36, so Barr regarded it as his proudest moment in baseball.

"It started against the Pirates at Candlestick," Barr said, "and the last guy to get on base was the pitcher, who got a hit to lead off the third inning. I got everybody out after that, including striking out Roberto Clemente to end the game.

"Then we went to St. Louis, and I got everybody out until two outs in the seventh, when Bernie Carbo hit a double. That stopped the streak at 41, and I didn't know what I had done. I just knew I had put two pretty good games back to back.

"I had a 2-0 count on Carbo and had to come in with a strike. I thought about throwing a slider, but decided on a fastball, thinking he might pop it up or ground out. The pitch was a little high. He doubled, but I got my second straight shutout."

And a record that still stands.

Breaking In with a Bang

Everyone steeped in Giants lore is aware of Willie McCovey's four-hit debut off Robin Roberts of the Phillies in 1959 and of Bobby Bonds's grand slam homer against the Dodgers in his first major-league game in 1968.

Dave Kingman made an equally imposing first impression when his first major-league game resulted in a pinch-hit grand slam against the Pirates in 1971. Suggesting it was no fluke, the rangy youngster clubbed two homers off Dock Ellis in his first start. Primarily an outfielder/first baseman, Kingman started his S.F. career as a third baseman "because I've got to get that bat of his in the lineup someplace," reasoned manager Charlie Fox, who had Willie McCovey at first base and plenty of outfielders.

The Greatest Comeback

In perhaps the most impressive comeback in San Francisco history, the Giants trailed the Pittsburgh Pirates 7-1 with two outs and a man on first base in the ninth inning at Candlestick Park, May 1, 1973, when they rallied for an 8-7 victory.

It was reminiscent of a nine-run ninth that fell short (11-10) against the Pirates in 1958 at Seals Stadium. But this one had a happy ending, thanks to a grand slam homer by utility man Chris Arnold and a three-run double by Bobby Bonds.

Bob Moose walked the bases full and was replaced by Ramon Hernandez, who fed pinch hitter Arnold a fat 3-2 pitch for the slam and 7-5. Gary Matthews doubled and Hernandez walked two batters before a Bonds double cleared the bases.

Hot Dog Or Hustler?

Tito Fuentes had a flamboyant style, making fancy backhand flips to shortstop Chris Speier on double plays and bouncing his bat off the plate while at bat. By some, he was labeled a "hot dog," which is not a term of endearment in baseball.

"I never understood why they didn't like me," a puzzled Fuentes said at the time. "Now, I think I know, now that they do like me. I think a man is a hot dog if he bounces around and doesn't play well.

"But if you do the same things and you are successful, then they compare you to Pete Rose and say you are a hustler. I think that is the difference between hot dogs and hustlers. I have to bounce around. I have too much energy."

Bobby's Big Day

Before there was Barry there was Bobby. And the elder Bonds perhaps enjoyed his finest day as a major-leaguer in the 1973 All-Star Game at Kansas City. It was a season in which the Giants' speedy slugger just missed 40-40 distinction with 39 home runs and 43 steals.

He also set a major-league record with 11 home runs as the leadoff batter, but was not among the starters at the All-Star Game. It didn't matter. After replacing right fielder Billy Williams in the fourth inning, Bobby belted a two-run homer off Bill Singer and later stretched a routine single into a double, pacing a 7-1 rout and earning MVP honors.

"Bonds is the best player in America," NL manager Sparky Anderson declared. Added NL coach Gene Mauch: "Bonds may be the best player in baseball today." There weren't many who disagreed with that assessment, including Bonds.

"In that particular year," he recalled, "I was the best player. I should have hit .300 every year, and maybe I would have if I didn't have to hit for power. But if I had to do it all over again, I'd do the same thing because my team needed power, and I always played for what my team needed."

End of an Era

When Horace Stoneham, his empire in decay and disarray, traded Bobby Bonds to the New York Yankees for Bobby Murcer, Oct. 22, 1974, it marked the final chapter in his systematic destruction of the Giants' star system. Bobby wasn't totally surprised, not after seeing Willie Mays, Juan Marichal, Willie McCovey and Gaylord Perry depart.

At the time of the first trade of $100,000 ballplayers it was reported that a heated argument between Bonds and Stoneham in the owner's office at Candlestick Park prefaced the trade. When Bonds left the meeting after speaking his mind, Stoneham supposedly declared: "He's finished—he'll never play another game for me."

After rejoining the Giants as batting coach in 1993, Bonds had a different version, recalling: "That argument never happened. I always got along with Mr. Stoneham. He just had his reasons and nobody ever told me why. But I got a big raise from the Yankees, so I didn't mind.

"If there was animosity over my leaving the Giants, it was because I knew we would have won if we had stayed together. They got rid of guys like George Foster, Garry Maddox and Gary Matthews. But those were hard times for Mr. Stoneham. After Mays, McCovey, Marichal and Perry were traded, we knew anyone could be traded."

On the surface, however, the Bonds-for-Murcer swap never made sense. At the time, each was 28, but Bonds was superior in virtually every phase of the game, holding an edge over Murcer in hits (1,106-1,002), runs (765-530), doubles (188-157), triples (42-28), homers (186-140), RBI (552-542), stolen bases (263-68) and producing superstar athletes (Barry).

A Beacon in the Fog

Things were bleak for the Giants in the mid-'70s when a financially strapped Horace Stoneham pared the roster of superstars like Willie Mays, Juan Marichal, Willie McCovey, Gaylord Perry and Bobby Bonds, along with promising youngsters like George Foster, Gary Matthews and Garry Maddox.

What made those years bearable was colorful right-hander John "The Count" Montefusco, who backed up his audacious boasts with some stellar pitching, including a no-hitter in 1976. When he made his debut at Dodger Stadium, Sept. 3, 1974, the former semipro gave an indication of what was to come.

"I got drunk the night before they called me up," Montefusco recalled. "I knew I was going up, but they told me I wouldn't pitch for at least a week. When I got to Dodger Stadium, it was the first time I'd been around major-leaguers. It was a thrill."

What the bleary-eyed Montefusco didn't expect was to be pitching right away. But the Dodgers loaded the bases with no outs off Ron Bryant in the first inning and manager Wes Westrum, in desperation, turned to the rookie.

"I was ready to turn around and walk out of there," Montefusco said. "As I walked to the mound, I was saying to myself, 'Well, here it is—do you belong here or don't you?' I was shaking, really nervous."

When Westrum attempted to calm him down, Montefusco told his manager that he was going to strike out the side. He came close. The first batter hit a grounder, but the next two struck out and The Count was out of the inning.

Better than that, he finished the game, yielding one run and striking out seven in nine innings. He also homered in the Giants' 9-5 victory, a perfect start for a brash youngster who "couldn't ask for anything better breaking into the big leagues."

Accepting a Challenge

Were it not for his stubbornness and showmanship, Montefusco might never have pitched his no-hitter in Atlanta, Sept. 29, 1976. He had been ill, so manager Bill Rigney asked if The Count might want to wait and start the next series in Houston instead.

But Montefusco had a habit of taunting certain hitters— Johnny Bench, Ron Cey and Reggie Smith among them—and he had made a promise that Willie Montanez wouldn't get a hit off him the rest of the season after the first baseman was traded from the Giants.

"It was our last game with the Braves that year, and I couldn't back down on that," Montefusco explained. "I had to go out there and at least give him a chance. I pitched to him in two games before that, and he was oh for seven."

Montanez, who had asked to be traded, was hitless that day, along with everyone else. He finished the season zero for 10 against The Count, who struck out four and walked one in possibly the most sparsely attended no-hitter in modern history: 1,369 paying customers.

"I felt pretty good warming up, and I'd just learned a sinker from Frank Funk," Montefusco said. "I decided to throw it in the game, and I don't know where I got the concentration from, but I was on for every single pitch to every single hitter for nine innings.

"I put the ball exactly where I wanted it. I didn't have real good stuff the first three innings, but I put the ball where I wanted. After that, when I knew I had the no-hitter going and I started getting my momentum and my good stuff, I knew I had them."

Ho-Ho's No-No

It was Aug. 24, 1975, and 24,175 were in the stands for the last no-hitter pitched at Candlestick Park by a Giant. It was rangy right-hander Ed Halicki's turn to shine, and "Ho-Ho" snuffed out the New York Mets, 6-0, with 10 strikeouts.

Second baseman Derrell Thomas was a key figure in the game, stealing three bases, scoring twice and making an error on a controversial play when Rusty Staub hit a ball off Halicki's leg and Thomas bobbled the pickup and threw late to first base.

"I was aware of it from about the fifth inning on, but I didn't think it would become a reality until the eighth inning when I saw I needed only six more outs," Halicki said. "In the last inning, I had to face Felix Millan, Mike Vail, Jesus Alou and Wayne Garrett.

"I knew Millan was a good contact hitter, and that if anybody was going to break up the no-hitter, I felt he was the guy. I ended up striking him out on a hanging slider, which I couldn't believe.

"Then I walked Vail and got two strikes on Alou. He fouled off about seven pitches and popped out to third. I think I threw

Garrett a breaking ball inside, and he hit a two-hopper to Willie Montanez at first, and that was it."

It's Only a Game

Eddie Bressoud once had a "vanity" license plate inscribed E-6, but fellow shortstop Johnnie LeMaster did even better at poking fun at himself. Responding to fans who booed him incessantly for subpar play, LeMaster had his name replaced on the back of his jersey with three letters: BOO.

The fans got a kick out of the self-deprecating stitching, but general manager Spec Richardson didn't appreciate the humor. He made LeMaster remove the unconventional identification and chastised him for the gesture.

Clark's Career Year

It didn't take Jack Clark long to have his career year with the Giants. In his first full major-league season, The Ripper flourished as the offensive leader of the 1978 resurgence at age 22. Pitching newcomer Vida Blue received the bulk of the credit, but Clark's contribution was significant.

He established two franchise records that season, hammering 46 doubles—a mark surpassed by Jeff Kent's 49 in 2001—and assembling a 26-game hitting streak that was prolonged by a successful pinch-hitting appearance, July 16, for 17 in a row. Clark batted .368 with 10 doubles, eight homers and 29 RBI during the streak, June 30-July 25.

In the process, he surpassed the previous franchise record of 24 straight games shared by Freddie Lindstrom, Don Mueller and Willie McCovey. And it wasn't a fluke. He earlier had a 19-game hitting streak the same year, batting .459.

"The bat feels like a magic wand—I shake it and it gets hits," was Clark's clever explanation of being in a groove. But his constant griping about Candlestick Park and his frustration over losing prefaced a trade to the St. Louis Cardinals in 1985.

The God Squad

The Giants caused quite a stir in the late 1970s with their born-again Christian movement that affected clubhouse harmony. The ringleader was relief ace Gary Lavelle, who didn't endear himself to some of the San Francisco populace with the final assessment.

"The Bay Area is the center of devil worship, radical groups and homosexuality in the country. It is a satanic region."

Shortly after Jack Clark became a born-again Christian, a Giant wondered aloud: "Why is it that Jack Clark can find God but not the cutoff man?"

A Save for Herseth

Although Bob Lurie was a major mover in twice keeping the Giants in San Francisco, it would not have happened in 1976 if a rich Arizona meatpacker named Bud Herseth didn't have an itch to get into major-league baseball.

When the Horace Stoneham regime crumbled and the National League temporarily took control of the club, Mayor George Moscone launched an effort to prevent the Giants from moving to Toronto and arranged for Lurie to join Bob Short of Minnesota as joint investors.

Short, however, because of his background as a former owner, insisted that he run the club. Lurie balked, and as the deadline for purchasing the Giants neared, NL owners applied the pressure on a noon teleconference call.

"I requested that I have 48 hours to find a new partner," Lurie said. "There was a little grumbling about that, so I asked for 24. They talked and said, 'We'll give you five hours. We've got to get this over with and let the club go to Toronto—the Bay Area can't support two teams.'

"Around 2:30, people who worked in the office were starting to panic. At about 2:45, Corey Busch, the mayor's press secretary calls and says, 'We've had a lot of nutty calls, but there's a guy in Arizona who says he's got $4 million, and we think he's for real.'

"So, approximately 15 to 20 phone calls later, to his bank and to people I knew in Arizona, at about 4:40 we had a verbal deal. I got on the phone and told the league we had a deal. The owners approved. Had Herseth not come through, the Giants would have been in Toronto."

A's Invasion Costly

When the Stoneham empire crumbled in the mid-1970s, it was convenient—and probably justified—to place the blame on the A's, who did business eight miles across the bay in Oakland. There was ample proof that Northern California would have difficulty supporting two major-league teams.

When Charles O. Finley received permission from American League owners to move his team from Kansas City in 1968, Stoneham was stunned to learn that he didn't have territorial rights. He thought he had paid for exclusivity in the growing Bay Area market.

"The only way Finley was able to get the shift approved was that the [AL] meetings kept stretching out longer and longer," Stoneham said. "Finally, one morning—it was about 3 a.m.— they approved the shift because they wanted to go to bed."

The impact of the A's was immediate. The Giants were contenders, yet their attendance plunged from 1,242,480 in 1967 to 837,220 in 1968. The A's drew an almost identical 837,466 that year. Oakland did more damage by winning three consecutive World Series in 1972-74 while the Stoneham franchise was in its demise.

When the A's move was announced on Oct. 18, 1967, Stoneham was asked for a response. It was both honorable and prophetic.

"Certainly, the move will hurt us," he said. "It's a question of whether both of us can survive. I don't think the area at the present time will take care of both of us as much as they [AL owners] think it will.

"We thought there'd always be only one club in this vicinity and that we'd be the one. It would appear we weren't far-sighted enough. He [Finley] did what he thought had to be done. And with the approval from his league, he had every right to do it."

A's Lend a Hand

There's no question that the success of the A's in the early 1970s was a thorn in the side, but Oakland owner Charles O. Finley was largely responsible for the Giants' resurgence in 1978 when he shipped Vida Blue across the bay for seven players.

Whereas none of the traded Giants made an impact with the A's, Blue was an immediate success, winning 18 games and making the pitching staff one of the most formidable in the National League.

"The beautiful part of the Vida Blue trade was that even though we gave up seven players, it didn't hurt our big-league club at all," said Joe Altobelli, who had the Giants in first place at the All-Star break and was named Manager of the Year.

Of course, Finley didn't do it out of kindness. He actually sold Blue to the Cincinnati Reds for $1.7 million, but the deal was voided by commissioner Bowie Kuhn, who invoked the "in the best interests of baseball" clause.

"As soon as the commissioner killed the A's deal with Cincinnati, I was on the phone to Charlie, telling him that if he wanted to trade Vida to keep us in mind," said general manager Spec Richardson. "He hung up on me the first time, but we had better young players to give up than other clubs."

So, moments before the March 15 interleague trading deadline, Blue was acquired for Gary Thomasson, Gary Alexander, Dave Heaverlo, Alan Wirth, John Johnson, Paul Huffman, Mario Guerrero and $400,000.

Heaverlo, Wirth, Johnson and Huffman, the four Giants pitching prospects involved, generally went on to mediocre success with Oakland. Blue posted 18 victories for S.F. in 1978 and Richardson was named Executive of the Year.

"Pure contentment—I never had so much fun in years," said Blue, who won a total of 72 games with the Giants. "Because of all the distractions, I couldn't even enjoy those World Series years with the A's. The [1978] team and the fans are really pumping me up."

Bryant's Bombshell

Ron Bryant's promising career as a Giant came to a sudden end two years after he led the National League in 1973 with a 24-12 record, the most wins in S.F. history by a left-hander. A swimming pool accident in Palm Springs the following spring required 30 stitches on his right side and lengthy hospitalization.

Bryant finished with a 3-15 record that season, and following spring training in 1975 he elected to forego his $50,000 salary to spend more time with his family.

"Mentally, I had trouble after that swimming pool thing," Bryant said. "It kind of preyed on my mind that the club had relied on me as a winner."

A Real Hot Bat

When Bobby Murcer was traded to the Giants from the Yankees for Bobby Bonds prior to the 1975 season, the Candlestick Park cold became a shock to his system. He performed well in his two San Francisco seasons, but he never became accustomed to the weather.

As a solution to the frigid conditions, he elected to reside on the other side of the East Bay hills, where the climate was much warmer. He also came up with a unique way to keep his bats warm—using the clubhouse sauna. Before coming to bat, Murcer would dispatch a batboy to fetch some heated lumber.

"The main reason I did it was because the bat wouldn't sting my hands when I made contact," he explained. "The only problem was that the pine tar on the handles melted right into the bat. And I moved to where it's warmer so I could have seven or eight hours between games to thaw out."

The '80s:
From Last to First in Two Seasons

Rosen, Craig Revive Giants
During Humm-Baby Years

The Longest Night

It was June 9, 1980, a damp Monday night in Philadelphia, when the Giants and Phillies made history and helped to bring about a curfew rules change. They endured a record five hours of rain delays at Veterans Stadium before San Francisco registered a 3-1 victory.

The lengthy wait occurred in the fourth inning, as the weary Giants trudged on after an early-morning wakeup call in Houston and a flight to Philadelphia for a game they didn't expect. It started at 7:35 p.m. and didn't end until 3:11 the next morning.

Steve Carlton had a no-hitter when it started pouring after the Giants were retired in the fourth inning. When play resumed in a drizzle following a 1:28 delay, Bob Boone homered off John Montefusco for the game's first run. With one out and one on, plate umpire Bob Engel again cleared the field, this time for an ungodly 3:32.

With a paid crowd of 28,702 in the stands and Carlton pitching a perfect game, Phillies owner Bill Giles kept giving the umpires an enthusiastic weather report. When the rain stopped, Giants reliever Allen Ripley was ordered to the mound, where he took his time warming up under orders from manager Dave Bristol.

"The Giants didn't want to play," Giles said. "They'd only had four hours of sleep before flying from Houston, and Carlton was pitching. Bristol was doing everything he could to stall, and I don't blame him."

Following another brief delay, play began at 1:28, the Giants tied it off Carlton in the fifth, and Jack Clark's two-run homer off Dickie Noles in the eighth made it 3-1. After Greg Minton saved the game for Ripley, he sighed with relief and summed up the mood of the club with: "I hope they leave a wakeup call for 4:30 in the afternoon."

Unlikely Hero

Ron Pruitt didn't have any significant playing time with the Giants, but shortly after he joined the club down the stretch in 1982, the seldom-used utility man delivered a clutch hit that made him an unlikely hero.

It was Sept. 30, 1982, and the Giants desperately needed a victory to remain one game out of first place entering the final weekend of the season. It didn't look good when Harry Spilman's second homer of the game gave the Houston Astros a 6-5 lead in the top of the ninth.

But in the bottom half, the Candlestick crowd erupted deliriously when Pruitt's first official at-bat as a Giant forged an improbable victory. His two-out bloop single to center scored two runs for a 7-6 victory, and teammates mobbed the sudden star. Pruitt finished his S.F. career with a mere five at-bats and two hits, and one was a big one.

"I've had pinch hits before, but never with this much on the line—this was the biggest," said Pruitt, who relished his Andy Warhol moment after languishing on the bench without an at-bat for three weeks.

The magic moment was set up by Darrell Evans's one-out walk. Jeff Leonard's two-out single kept the rally going, and pinch hitter Jim Wohlford walked off Dave Smith, loading the bases. Then Pruitt batted for Johnnie LeMaster and delivered on a 3-1 pitch.

Upping the Ante

Duane Kuiper had a good relationship with Frank Robinson, who was his manager in Cleveland and San Francisco. Kuiper enjoyed watching Robby interact with other players, and there was a particularly memorable exchange with equally stubborn Reggie Smith on a team bus following a tough loss in 1982.

"Reggie's on the back of the bus, and he's ragging on Frank's managing in this game," Kuiper recalled. "Frank's sitting in the front seat, and Reggie is talking loud enough so Frank would hear him. He gets the drift and says, 'That'll be $100, Reggie!' Reggie snaps back, 'Make it $200!'

"Frank complies and tells Reggie, 'Go as long as you like.' "They keep going back and forth until it gets to $1900, and then it finally stops. Neither one of them wanted to give in. Frank collected all of it, too."

Not So Fast

Frank Robinson wasn't someone to take any guff. The Hall of Famer played the game on the edge, and he managed the same way. His feisty nature became readily apparent one day at Shea Stadium when Robinson went to remove Jim Barr from the mound.

Barr was upset, so he headed for the dugout before the manager reached the mound. Robinson, not one to be shown up, grabbed Barr, spun him around and emphatically escorted him back to the mound before taking the ball.

"J. B. was ticked off because Frank had told him to pitch Dave Kingman carefully, and then Frank comes out of the dugout after Kingman walks," recalled Duane Kuiper, who was playing second base at the time.

"He started to walk off the mound before Frank got there, and I turned to [shortstop] Johnnie LeMaster and told him, 'This is not good.' I knew how Frank would react, and he locks arms with J. B. like they were doing a polka and practically lifted him to the mound."

Barr was stunned by Robinson's show of strength, and the manager admitted when he returned to the dugout in 2002 that he had mellowed and "would have handled the situation differently now—I'd have dealt with it in private instead of in front of everybody."

Moon Man's Caper

Reliever Greg Minton is credited with being one of the zaniest players in S.F. history. He was a prankster, but didn't resort to common antics like hotfoots. The aptly named Moon Man enjoyed his fun on a larger scale.

During a 1982 trip to Houston, Minton climbed into the team bus parked outside the club's hotel and told the driver the rest of the players already had departed for the Astrodome.

He convinced the perplexed driver to take him to the ballpark, assuring him no other players were relying on a busride. Minton was laughing gleefully as angry teammates arrived by taxi and trickled into the clubhouse.

"I enjoyed that," he said. "Some of the guys were mad, but then they realized it was just Moonie having some fun. I thought it was unique. Nobody got hurt, and we won 13 out of 15 after that."

On the Serious Side

One reason Minton's 1982 tomfoolery was tolerated probably coincided with his career year as a major-league pitcher. He posted a franchise-record 30 saves, accompanied by a 10-4 record and a 1.83 ERA with a devastating sinker.

The performance earned him a million-dollar contract, a reward for his stellar work since replacing injured Randy Moffitt as the right-handed stopper. From Sept. 6, 1978, to May 2, 1982, Minton set a major-league record of 269 and one-third innings without yielding a home run.

"I'm a sinkerball pitcher, and you're not supposed to give up homers if you keep the ball low," Minton said after John Stearns of the New York Mets ended the streak at Candlestick Park. "It's really no big deal.

"Stearns got a fastball, up and in the strike zone. I thought about tackling him as he rounded third, but then I remembered that he's strong and once played football."

What's in a Name?

When the Giants traded slugger Jack Clark to the St. Louis Cardinals prior to the 1985 season, they received infielder Jose Gonzalez along with pitcher Dave LaPoint and first baseman Gary Rajsich. Gonzalez proved to be the best of the newcomers, landing the shortstop job for two division champions.

But Jose never appeared in a Giants' box score under that name. He first changed to Uribe Gonzalez, taking his mother's maiden name as his first. Then he decided there were too many Gonzalezes playing ball, so he finally settled on Jose Uribe.

That prompted coach Rocky Bridges's classic quip: "Jose truly was the player to be named later."

Penitentiary Face

Outfielder Jeff Leonard's gruff demeanor earned him the nickname "Penitentiary Face" from teammate Bob Brenly. He wasn't always that grouchy, but he encouraged the reputation by frequently demonstrating his rough edges.

Late in his Giants career, however, Leonard was known more as "Hac-Man" or "Hac," and he wanted to soften his image. He requested that he be called Jeffrey instead of Jeff because it sounded more formal.

The sportswriters covering the club complied, calling him Jeffrey at the height of his career, when he helped the club to a division title and was MVP of the 1987 NLCS. But they also made his nickname more formal, so "Penitentiary Face" was changed to "Correctional Institution Face."

The Crazy Crab

When the Giants were going badly in the early 1980s, their fans were in no mood for a mascot. Envious of the Philly Phanatic and the San Diego Chicken, management decided to introduce a comic crustacean called the Crazy Crab.

Big mistake. C. C. was an object of derision from the start. Whenever he appeared, fans booed lustily. The marketing wizards finally got the message when the Giants' players turned on Crazy Crab, whose career mercifully was short-lived.

"We started playing games with him," pitcher Bill Laskey recalled. "We'd put heat [ointment] inside the armpits, so it got pretty warm when he put on the outfit. The guys in the bullpen turned hoses on him and threw baseballs at him. It was a mascot that was never forgotten—and never understood."

Added Greg Minton: "Crazy Crab stood out. The fans hated him, and the players hated him, but I felt sorry for him because people would boo and moon him—including some players."

A Corking Good Time

When good-humored Bob Brenly was asked about allegations that Pete Rose used a corked bat en route to a hits record, Brenly didn't say that Rose would never cheat, but he suggested that the Giants might have during his days as their catcher in the 1980s.

"We had a professional cabinet maker/woodworker on our staff in San Francisco," he recalled with a smile. "I'm sure he wasn't there to hang jocks. I've played with some of the best and most notorious bat-corkers of all time—guys who turned it into an art form. They should have hung some of those bats in a museum.

"Let's put it this way. One of the keys to corking a bat is you have to drill a hole down the middle of the bat into the hitting area. Then you pack it with pieces of chopped cork as tightly as you can. The key is the plug you put back in at the end of the bat.

"I played with a guy who saved the last inch and one-half of dozens of broken bats. When he was ready to plug that hole, he would take all the little caps and match them up so the grain lined up exactly perfect with the plug. That's a master craftsman."

A Strikeout Spree

Nobody was blown off the mound when the All-Star Game returned to Candlestick Park following a 23-year absence in 1984, but plenty of hitters were blown away in a record strikeout spree at the 55th Midsummer Classic.

"The twilight might have been a factor," said American League manager Joe Altobelli after a record 21 batters whiffed in a 3-1 National League victory before 57,756. It was the winners' 20th triumph in 22 games.

Fernando Valenzuela and Dwight Gooden combined for six straight strikeouts in the fourth and fifth innings to erase Carl Hubbell's record five in a row, 50 years to the day. And the strikeout splurge came without absent Steve Carlton and Nolan Ryan, one-two on the all-time list.

Goose Gossage worked the ninth inning and struck out Eddie Murray and Rickey Henderson for the record total, erasing the previous mark of 20 in 1968. Gary Carter was the MVP for a game-winning homer and a run-saving block at home plate.

Painting the Town Orange

Mike Krukow, Duane Kuiper and Steve Nicosia started a rookie hazing ritual one day when the Giants' team bus was heading from the club's downtown Chicago hotel to Wrigley Field in 1984. The bus passed a statue of General Sheridan after turning off Lakeshore Drive, and the three veterans thought it would be a good idea if the underside of the general's horse had some color.

They convinced rookies Jeff Cornell and Frank Williams to do the deed with some bright orange paint, and the sight elicited uproarious laughter from the rest of the team when the bus took the same route the next day.

"It's become a tradition around the league, and every team has its own interpretation, but we were the first," Krukow proudly claimed. "It really got serious in 1986 because we had a ton of rookies on the team, guys like Will Clark, Robby Thompson and Bob Melvin.

"We're going to Wrigley one day, and as we pass the statue, I get up on the bus and make this speech about Giants tradition. I was fired up, telling the rookies that this was a ticket to a 10-year contract and gaining acceptance."

The fiery speech worked. That night, traveling secretary Dirk Smith made arrangements for the team bus to pick up the large contingent of eager rookies, each brandishing a brush and paint. Krukow went along for the ride.

"It was amazing," he said. "We had a big group of guys all over that statue, and they really did a job. They came back on the bus with paint all over themselves, and I told them they missed a spot, so they went and did it again.

"The upshot was that we had a Bay Area TV crew filming a documentary on the club. They asked if they could come along, and I told them OK on the condition they would just make copies for us and not air it.

"When we get back to San Francisco, [general manager] Al Rosen calls me into his office and reads me the riot act. He was hot, telling me he turned on the TV and all he saw was drunkeness and vandalism. It was difficult to keep from laughing."

As the years went by, the prank became more sophisticated. A former Cubs batboy working for the Chicago vice squad rounded up some of his meanest sidekicks to enter the Giants' clubhouse the next day and make mock arrests. At that point, many of the rookies no longer were laughing, but Krukow and the rest of the team were.

Rookie Initiation, Part Two

As if the paint-a-thon weren't enough to initiate Giants rookies, there was another rite involving inexpensive and gaudy shoes purchased whenever the club visited Atlanta, which was three times a year before realignment.

"Anyone called up to the club had to go through it, so nobody got out of it," Krukow explained. "The shoes would cost about $20, and the store had a section for entertainers, so you had shiny patent leather jobs in all sorts of bright colors with raised heels.

"When getaway day came, we'd take the rookies' shoes and replace them with the loud ones in their lockers. They had no choice but to wear them, and it was quite a sight when they walked through the airport. On some teams, they did it with the whole wardrobe. I remember a guy going home in a wedding dress."

Quick-Thinking Rookie

During the 1986 season, rookie left-hander Terry Mulholland made a memorable play in a September game with the New York Mets. It was the third inning, and Keith Hernandez hit a grounder to the right side. It was hit so hard, it stuck in the pitcher's glove.

Unable to dislodge the ball and running out of time, Mulholland alertly took the glove off and lobbed it to stunned first baseman Bob Brenly, who grabbed it for the out. The Mets protested, but the umpire correctly made the out call on a weird play.

Talkin' Baseball

The Giants added to their collection of Hall of Fame players when left-hander Steve Carlton joined the club briefly in 1986. But the all-time strikeout leader (at the time) was out of character in a San Francisco uniform—he talked.

"It's been 10 years since I've done this, so pardon me if I make any mistakes," Carlton began his 15-minute opening press conference. "You cannot make a move like this and not talk to the media. I can't say if it will continue in the future. We will discuss nothing about the past. I haven't talked for 10 years, and that's the way I liked it."

Jeffrey Leonard, predictably gruff, playfully snapped: "If he talks, I talk! I'll tell you one thing, the man [Carlton] already is in the book for not being dressed for batting practice. We don't play no favorites here."

A Dream Comes True

When Mike Krukow posted an 11-2 victory at Dodger Stadium on the final day of the 1986 season, it punctuated a 21-game improvement by the Giants and made him the club's first 20-game winner since Ron Bryant in 1973. It also made him wonder if teammate Candy Maldonado was psychic.

"We were talking one day this summer," Krukow recalled, "and Candy told me, 'You're going to win 20 and I'm going to clinch it with a grand slam in L.A.' He really said it."

Maldonado did even better. He drove in six runs against his former team, and there indeed was a grand slam among his two home runs.

"I had a dream it was going to happen here," Candy confirmed Krukow's story. "But I didn't predict a grand slam. I just said I hoped it was a grand slam."

Brenly Bobbles Blasts

Catcher Bob Brenly was playing out of position against the Atlanta Braves at Candlestick Park, Sept. 14, 1986, and it showed. He tied a major-league record with four errors in the fourth inning at third base, placing the Giants in a 4-0 holes.

But Brenly redeemed himself gloriously in a remarkable personal comeback. He homered in the fifth, and his two-run single created a 6-6 tie in the seventh. Then his two-out homer off Paul Assenmacher in the bottom of the ninth gave the Giants a sweet 7-6 victory.

"This isn't your typical storybook finish—it's a novel!" Mike Krukow shrieked in the clubhouse. Manager Roger Craig, who switched Brenly to catcher in the eighth inning, declared: "This is the greatest Humm-Baby game of the year!"

Brenly was happy, too, especially because he was saved more embarrassment by moving behind the plate.

"I went from the outhouse to the penthouse," he quipped. "I was the Comeback Player of the Year in one afternoon. When Roger told me to catch, I thanked him. I didn't want to see another ground ball. I can laugh about it now, but I wasn't too pleased about the four errors at the time.

"It was frustrating, and I was supposed to start the game as the catcher. But Chris Brown showed up with a sprained eyelash, or something like that, so I'm at third base hoping they would hit the ball to somebody else. That game was like an out-of-body experience."

A Giant Jolt

Long before the devastating earthquake delayed the 1989 World Series, the Giants learned that Mother Nature and their championship seasons go hand in hand. It was the final weekend of the 1987 season, and the Giants were playing in Los Angeles after clinching the division title in San Diego.

An earthquake that registered 6.1 on the Richter Scale jolted them out of bed on the morning of Oct. 1. It was the strongest quake in Southern California since 1971, which incidentally was the year the Giants won their first division championship.

"That's as helpless as I've ever felt," manager Roger Craig said before leaving the hotel and heading to Dodger Stadium for a nap. "This was the worst. I looked for the hotel walls to come down."

Gallows humor helped some players relax. Pitcher Mike LaCoss, for instance, phoned travelling secretary Dirk Smith shortly after the earthquake hit and said: "Hello, Dirk. I have a complaint about my room. It keeps shaking and I'm having trouble sleeping."

When the downtown hotel was evacuated, the Giants poured onto the street, many of them in sartorial disarray. Veteran equipment manager Mike Murphy was nattily attired in his usual shirt and tie—but he was standing on the sidewalk barefooted.

The Clincher

How fitting it was that on Sept. 28, 1987, Dave Dravecky started and Don Robinson finished a division-clinching 5-4 victory in San Diego. Moreover, it was Robinson's solo homer off Lance McCullers in the seventh inning that provided the winning run.

"That's the stuff you dream about in the backyard playing wiffleball," an amazed Mike Krukow said of Robinson, who didn't expect to be summoned in relief and admittedly didn't have his best stuff.

Recalled Robinson: "I was in the bullpen without my knee brace on or my shoes tied. I threw only nine pitches. I wasn't ready. But the only thing on my mind when I came over here was to help this team win a pennant. It feels great."

After each team scored in the third inning, Mark Leonard's two-run homer in the top of the fourth placed the Giants ahead. But Randy Ready's homer and Tony Gwynn's run-scoring single made it 3-3 in the bottom half.

Chili Davis's homer—the 100th of his career—off ex-Giant Mark Davis in the fifth, placed the Giants ahead to stay before Robinson's homer made it 5-3. The Padres scored in the bottom of the seventh on a triple by rookie Benito Santiago, who extended his hitting streak to 30 games and 15 years later would be the Giants' playoff MVP.

Some Letdown

The first-place Giants were giddy following a four-game sweep of the Houston Astros, so a letdown was expected when they took the field, June 23, 1987, against the San Diego Padres. Some letdown. They clobbered the Padres 18-1 in one of the most decisive victories in their history.

What was amazing was that Giants starter Mike LaCoss maintained his focus and finished with a complete-game three-hitter. What was even more amazing was that Padres pinch-hitting specialist Dane Iorg pitched the eighth inning and surrendered home runs to LaCoss and Mike Woodard, the first major-league homers for both.

"I can throw strikes—I proved it today," Iorg said. But the Giants placed the game out of reach long before he took over, scoring five runs with seven of their 21 hits in the first inning. "It was like batting practice," Woodard said. "They gave me the game ball, but I'm going to hide it in the back of my locker. This one will have an asterisk by it."

Curiously, the rout wasn't the most decisive victory that day, Long after the Giants' matinee concluded, the host Philadelphia Phillies erupted for a 19-1 thumping of the Chicago Cubs.

Mother of All Comebacks

Manager Roger Craig, sensing he was having a bad dream, pulled a lot of his starters at Cincinnati, Sept. 4, 1989, when the Reds rolled to an 8-0 lead after six innings. By the time the game ended, the Reds' manager called it "a nightmare" because the Giants' reserves had rallied for an improbable 9-8 victory.

"We were just trying to get everybody some playing time and keep the regulars rested," explained seldom-used first baseman Mike Laga, who replaced Will Clark and produced two hits and three RBI in the stirring comeback while the veterans were cheering deliriously on the bench.

It all started with solo homers by Will Clark and Terry Kennedy in the seventh inning, but that didn't convince Craig to keep them in the game. Mike Laga and Bill Bathe replaced them and became a factor. Ernest Riles's two-out single and Laga's homer on his first Giants at-bat made it 8-4 in the eighth.

Then Norm Charlton, John Franco and Rob Dibble corroded in the five-run ninth. Pinch hitter Greg Litton and Donnell Nixon opened with singles and Bob Brenly was safe on an error, loading the bases. Pinch hitter Chris Speier singled for 8-5, and Bathe's two-run single made it a one-run game.

Scott Garrelts ran for Bathe, and Riles greeted Dibble with a single for the tie. With Clark and Kennedy whooping it up in street clothes in the tunnel to the dugout, Laga grounded a single through the hole on the right side and the comeback was complete.

"I'll never forget that game," said Craig, who exhausted his 25-man roster in a stunning victory that symbolized the team effort that produced a division championship.

Seeing Is Believing

A misty-eyed crowd of 34,810 gathered at Candlestick Park, Aug. 10, 1988, and it really had little to do with the Giants hosting the Cincinnati Reds. The emotional outpouring was for Dave Dravecky's return to the mound following cancer surgery.

What was unexpected was the manner in which Dravecky performed, as if nothing had happened. Through seven innings, he limited the Reds to one hit, a second-inning double by Joel Youngblood, and was staked to a 4-0 lead with the help of Matt Williams's homer and three RBI.

"The highlight today was to be able to stand on the mound and give thanks to almighty God for the miracle that enabled me to perform," said Dravecky, who was lifted following Luis Quinones's three-run homer in the ninth and was a 4-3 winner.

Manager Roger Craig shook his head in disbelief and said: "When I first saw his arm, I didn't think he'd ever pick up a baseball again. I've seen a lot of things in baseball, but I can't remember a game with more drama than this one."

A Tragedy in Montreal

Following his stirring return, Dave Dravecky made his next start against the Montreal Expos, Aug. 15, 1988, at Olympic Stadium. This time, there was heartache instead of happiness. He suffered a stress fracture of his left humerus and never pitched again.

With Tim Raines at the plate in the bottom of the sixth, Dravecky threw a fateful wild pitch, tumbled to the ground in excruciating pain, and was carried off on a stretcher and taken to Queen Elizabeth Hospital.

"It's unfair," manager Roger Craig said, fighting back tears. "It's like it was an act of God, but it was an act of God just for him to be out there. If this doesn't inspire a ballclub, nothing will. They had fire in their eyes."

Following a two-run Matt Williams homer in a 3-2 victory that made Dravecky 2-0, there was an encouraging report that no surgery would be required and that the healing process would take six to eight weeks.

"I had the feeling that he would never pitch again," said catcher Terry Kennedy, who sadly was proven correct. On Oct. 9, the arm was broken again in the Giants' pennant-winning celebration; in November, a cancerous lump was found in Dravecky's arm, and it was eventually amputated.

A One-Two Punch

Career years coincided for Kevin Mitchell and Will Clark in 1989, and their efforts were rewarded by a one-two finish in the MVP race, something that hadn't happened since Joe Morgan and George Foster did it with the Cincinnati Reds. Mitchell received 20 of the 24 first-place votes; Clark had three firsts and 15 seconds.

"I'm very shocked," said Mitchell, who batted .291 with 47 home runs and 125 RBI. "It means a lot. I never won anything in my life. Will was great. He helped me out a lot. We were like batteries to each other."

Clark, who was to become the Giants' NLCS hero, finished with a career-high .333 average, losing the batting title to Tony Gwynn on the final day of the season. He also had 38 doubles, nine triples, 23 home runs and 111 RBI.

The '90s:
Bonds, New Owners to the Rescue

Giants Stay Home, Bring New Era of Success

A Good Start

It didn't take long for Dusty Baker to register his first of 840 victories as the Giants' manager. On Opening Day, April 6, 1993, John Burkett pitched six strong innings and newcomer Barry Bonds knocked in the winning run in a 2-1 victory over the St. Louis Cardinals.

"I'm glad it didn't take as long for the first one as it did in spring training, when we were 0-4," a thankful Baker said. "Close games here usually go to the Cardinals, so it's nice to get away with one."

A Busch Stadium crowd of 50,269 watched Burkett and Bob Tewksbury match shutouts until Dave Martinez's double and Will Clark's two-out single hoisted the Giants to a 1-0 lead in the fourth inning.

After the Cardinals tied it in the sixth on a walk and Ozzie Smith's triple, a great fielding play by shortstop Royce Clayton prevented the go-ahead run. Clark's double, Smith's error, and Bonds's sacrifice fly produced the game-winning RBI in his Giants debut.

Bonds's Homecoming

For years, Giants' fans became accustomed to Will Clark's flair for the dramatics. They quickly discovered that Bonds had the same quality when the new left fielder homered on his first at-bat as a Giant at Candlestick Park, triggering a 4-3 victory over the Florida Marlins.

A record crowd of 56,689 watched Bonds deliver off Chris Hammond with one out in the second inning. Royce Clayton followed with a single, and Mike Benjamin's homer gave Trevor Wilson a 3-0 lead he could not hold.

After the Marlins erupted for three runs in the sixth with a two-out rally that featured Benito Santiago's two-run homer, the Giants won it in the 11th on Benjamin's single, winner Rod Beck's sacrifice, Willie McGee's intentional walk and Darren Lewis's single.

A Pinch of Patterson

The Giants' euphoria over Thompson's homer swiftly ebbed when the Braves swept a three-game series at Candlestick to slice the lead to four and one-half games. And when the Braves won the opener of a three-game set in Atlanta, Aug. 31, the lead dwindled to three and one-half games and another sweep seemed possible.

That became more likely when Jeff Blauser's sixth-inning double gave the Braves a 2-1 lead behind John Smoltz. But Jeff Reed's double and Dave Martinez's single made it 2-2 in the seventh, setting up more Giants dramatics.

Baker needed a pinch hitter for pitcher Mike Jackson, so he glanced down his bench and spotted rookie John Patterson, just promoted from Triple-A Phoenix. With Mark Wohlers throwing heat, Patterson made his first major-league at-bat of the season memorable, homering over the right field bullpen for a 3-2 lead that Rod Beck preserved.

"I've been thinking about this at-bat every day," said Patterson, who would hit only four more homers in a brief Giants career. "In the back of my mind, I said, 'If the race gets tight, they're going to need another left-handed bat.' I never let that perspective get out of my head. That's what motivated me."

Patterson's pinch homer prevented the Braves from a sweep, but they made it five out of six the next night for a three and one-half-game deficit that set up a dazzling race to the wire. Summed up Baker: "The cavalry got here just in time."

Somebody, Please Help

When the Giants pulled into a tie with the Atlanta Braves on the final day of the 1993 season, rookie manager Dusty Baker asked for some help in deciding on a starting pitcher for that crucial game at Dodger Stadium.

"I'll pray on it like I always do," Baker said on the eve of the game. "I'll pray on it and ask the good Lord to help me make the right decision. I just wouldn't mind Him hurrying up."

With a choice of Scott Sanderson and Jim Deshaies, two veterans at the end of their careers, or rookie Salomon Torres, Baker went with the talented prospect. He was hammered, along with relievers Dave Burba and Dave Righetti, in a 12-1 loss that left the Giants with a 103-59 record and home for the playoffs. Atlanta finished 104-58.

So much for divine intervention.

Matt's Bad Timing

Despite Barry Bonds's presence, Matt Williams was the most productive Giants batter in 1994-95, but was plagued by ill fortune in the form of a work stoppage in 1994 and a foul tip off his foot one year later.

At the time of the strike in August of 1994, Williams had an incredible 43 home runs in 114 games, which projected to 61 over a full season, exactly Roger Maris's record at the time. The strike lopped 48 games off the Giants' schedule and another 18 games when the 1995 season started late following the replacement fiasco.

When play resumed in 1995, Williams was leading the National League with 13 home runs and 35 RBI while batting .381 in 36 games before fracturing a foot on a foul tip, June 3. Adding his 1995 start to his 1994 finish, he had 56 homers and 131 RBI in 150 games.

"I don't look back at it as wasted opportunity," Williams said. "I'd never hit that many home runs, so I don't know what I would have done if there wasn't a strike. My home runs will come, but I don't try to hit them."

Benji's Batting Binge

Mike Benjamin had a long career as a utility infielder because of his competence afield, but in a 1995 series with the Chicago Cubs, "Benji" enjoyed his Andy Warhol moment of fame as a major-leaguer, and it lasted three days instead of 15 minutes.

With a career batting average of .185, he astounded himself and the Giants by hitting six in one game, joining Jesus Alou as merely the second player to do so in S.F. history. Benjamin went on to register 14 hits in three games, a major-league record.

Playing third base for the injured Matt Williams, Benjamin had four hits, June 11, in a homestand finale. It was regarded as a fluke, but "Benji" had four more hits to pace an 8-4 victory over the Chicago Cubs at Wrigley, June 13.

"Give him all the credit," manager Dusty Baker said. "He's had less playing time than anyone, but he continued to work hard, and he's getting better pitches to hit batting ahead of Barry Bonds."

For an encore, Benjamin did even better. The next day, he tied Jesus Alou's S.F. record with six hits, including a run-scoring single in the 13th inning that produced a 4-3 win. For the three games, he went 14 for 18. The previous three-game record was 13 hits by Joe Cronin (1933), Walt Dropo (1952) and Tim Salmon (1994).

Declared Baker: "I've been around some great hitters—guys like Aaron, Cepeda, Carty and Garvey—but I've never seen anything like this. I'm totally amazed."

So was Benjamin, who was limited to merely one hit in a 3-1 loss to the Cubs, June 15. But it was a big one. Right-hander Frank Castillo had a perfect game until Benjamin lined a 2-2 pitch to center with one out in the seventh inning.

"It's hard to believe, you don't think it's realistic—I can't explain it," said Benjamin, somewhat embarrassed by the commotion. "I found my mind wandering because of all the attention. What ever happened to just playing the game?"

An Interleague First

The Giants had the distinction of starting the historic first interleague game, June 12, 1997, at The Ballpark at Arlington, and seemed to enjoy the American League variety of baseball in a 4-3 victory over the Texas Rangers.

Darryl Hamilton, a former Ranger, led off the game with the first interleague hit, a single off Darren Oliver. Stan Javier hit the first home run, tagging Oliver in the third inning for a 1-1 tie.

Texas went ahead with two runs in the sixth off winner Mark Gardner, but the Giants won it in a three-run seventh. Jose Vizcaino and Jeff Kent opened with singles, and Barry Bonds was hit by a pitch, loading the bases.

Mark Lewis's single and Glenallen Hill's sacrifice fly produced a tie. Javier's double pushed the Giants ahead to stay. Will Clark singled in three at-bats against his former team, and the game was played in an NL-style 2:23.

"All the butterflies are gone now," Bonds said following a double in three at-bats. "It takes time to get the feel of something. After they got the lead on us, we got aggressive."

Bay Area Bombshells

On July 31, 1997, the Giants and the A's both beat the trading deadline with blockbuster trades. But whereas Oakland dumped salary in allowing Mark McGwire to reach glory with the St. Louis Cardinals, S.F. pulled a heist in snatching pitchers Wilson Alvarez, Roberto Hernandez and Danny Darwin from the Chicago White Sox.

"I still can't believe it to a certain extent," rookie general manager Brian Sabean conceded after sending pitcher Ken Foulke and minor leaguers Mike Caruso, Brian Manning, Lorenzo Barcelo, Bobby Howry and Ken Vining to Chicago in what was termed the "White Flag Sale" in the Windy City.

Manager Dusty Baker agreed with Sabean, adding: "I couldn't believe it. I couldn't believe we were getting guys of this quality." The trade bolstered the Giants' pitching to the point where the club won its first division title in eight years. Alvarez won four games and Hernandez went 5-2 with four saves down the stretch as the club edged the Dodgers by two games.

He Did It Again

Brian Johnson's 12th-inning homer that enabled the Giants to catch the Dodgers in the 1997 stretch drive figured to be a tough act to follow. But on Sept. 24 at Coors Field, the catcher performed his magic again. This time, his tie-breaking homer in the top of the ninth downed the Colorado Rockies 4-3.

"Pure ecstasy," Johnson declared after his repeat performance gave the Giants a two and one-half-game lead over the Dodgers with three to play. "You always dream about hitting game-winning homers, but you don't expect them."

J. T. Snow and Roberto Hernandez also played significant roles. Snow hit his 28th home run and tied the game with an eighth-inning triple for 101 RBI before Johnson connected off a 1-2 Steve Reed fastball for his 11th Giants homer in merely 171 at-bats. Hernandez worked two hitless innings for the win.

An Immediate Hit

Jeff Kent made sure the Giants got the best of the deal by acquiring him and three others from the Cleveland Indians for Matt Williams by enjoying his first career year with 29 home runs and 121 RBI in 1997. Placing that in perspective, no other second baseman in S.F. history remotely came close to that production.

Before Kent, the best season by an S.F. second baseman was 19 home runs and 65 RBI by predecessor Robby Thompson in 1993. In fact, all six of Kent's seasons with the Giants greatly improved on Thompson's numbers.

By the time his Giants career came to an end shortly after the 2002 World Series, Kent had accumulated 175 home runs and 689 RBI in six S.F. seasons. Only Willie Mays had more consecutive 100-RBI seasons than Kent's six. And over the same six-year period, the oft-injured Williams mustered 117 home runs and 470 RBI.

A steal of a deal.

Neifi Nips Nen

With the Mets eliminated in a 7-3 loss to the Braves and the Astros edging the Cubs 4-3, all the Giants needed was a victory to grab the 1998 wild card and enjoy a two-day rest before opening the playoffs in Atlanta. One couldn't blame them for visualizing tomahawk chops when Joe Carter's two-run homer and Barry Bonds's double and triple helped to build a 7-0 lead in the top of the fifth.

But in what must go down as one of their more excruciating defeats, the horrified Giants watched the Rockies chip away against Kirk Rueter and four relievers. Ex-Giants Kirt Manwaring and Darryl Hamilton singled in a six-run bottom of the fifth that featured rookie Todd Helton's three-run homer and Neifi Perez's two-run triple.

Perez's single and Vinny Castilla's homer placed the Rockies ahead in the seventh, but in the eighth Jeff Kent homered off Pedro Astacio to tie the game. Not for long. Seconds after learning of the Cubs' loss, elation turned to dismay when Perez knocked Nen's 0-1 fastball into the right field seats.

"You should be in good shape with a seven-run lead, but if you told me last week that we'd earn a one-game playoff with the Cubs, we'd have been jumping up and down," GM Brian Sabean said. Added Baker: "There's no sadness on this team. We could be going home to paint the garage."

Irony Over Dustiny

What a cruel irony it was for the Giants in a one-game wild-card playoff, Sept. 28, 1998, at Wrigley Field. Cubs closer Rod

Beck, who called the 1997 Giants "a team of Dustiny" and was summarily replaced by Robb Nen as the club's bullpen ace, exacted revenge by knocking his former team out of the playoffs.

The Cubs rode Steve Trachsel's impeccable one-hit pitching to a 5-0 lead entering the top of the ninth when the Giants suddenly stirred against Kevin Tapani and Terry Mulholland. It started when consecutive singles by Brent Mayne, Bill Mueller and Stan Javier produced a run.

Pinch hitter Ellis Burks walked, loading the bases, and Barry Bonds hit a sacrifice fly. Beck replaced Mulholland and Jeff Kent's force grounder scored Javier for 5-3. Then Joe Carter, representing the tying run in what would be his final major-league at-bat, fouled to first baseman Mark Grace for a 5-3 victory and Beck's club-record 51st save.

"It's not about beating the Giants—it's about beating someone and getting to the playoffs," said Beck, who credited a tip from Baker for retiring Carter the first time he'd ever faced him. "I remember Dusty telling me when hitters have long arms, you throw them off-speed stuff insided. You don't want them to extend."

Curiously, Beck also holds the franchise saves record with the Giants, notching 48 in 1993. He remained close to Baker while rehabilitating from elbow surgery and rejoined Baker and the Cubs in spring training of 2003.

Out With the Old

Peter Magowan had lots of help, of course, but he will go down in history as the man who saved the Giants for San Francisco and moved them from dreaded Candlestick Park to gleaming Pacific Bell Park. Magowan was certain the team was doomed in Northern California without a new stadium.

"The team would have been put up for sale and sold, and the buyer would have been from out of the area and National League baseball would have disappeared forever," he said in 1999, describing Candlestick as "a stadium of concrete on a cul-de-sac with symmetrical dimensions and chain-link fences.

"The only thing that gave it any character was the weather, the elements. What was special about Candlestick other than the wind? From an architectural point of view, there is nothing to characterize it as unique. That's what makes a great ballpark, and our new ballpark will have a lot of things that will be very special.

"It will be a ballpark people will want to come to in 30, 40 years. We almost moved twice, in 1976 and 1992, and the A's almost moved at least twice. People can now fall in love with the Giants because they're going to be here for the long term, and that's a statement we couldn't make in the past."

A Sneak Preview

Not many exhibitions attract 40,930, but March 31, 2000, was something special for Giants fans—the unofficial opening of Pacific Bell Park. The demand was so great for that historic occasion that many more tickets could have been sold, and those who were fortunate soaked in the festive atmosphere of an 8-3 victory over the Milwaukee Brewers.

Kirk Rueter threw the first pitch at 7:39 p.m., and Brewers leadoff batter Marquis Grissom, who would become a Giant in three years, promptly doubled and scored the first run on Jose Hernandez's two-out single. Geoff Jenkins and ex-Giant Charlie Hayes also singled for a 2-0 lead.

The Giants tied it off Jimmy Haynes in the bottom half on Marvin Benard's triple, Bill Mueller's walk, Barry Bonds's double, and Jeff Kent's grounder and took the lead for good on Kent's walk and J. T. Snow's double in the fifth inning. There was even more commotion the next day because the Yankees were making their first visit since 1962.

An anxious crowd of 40,930 showed up, and Bonds immediately gave them something to cheer with the first home run at Pac Bell, a first-inning drive off Andy Pettitte. Ex-Yankee Russ Davis homered twice for the Giants, but Jorge Posada, Paul O'Neill and Roberto Kelly went deep for New York in an 11-6 victory.

"I had very high expectations, very high expctations, but this has exceeded them all," owner Peter Magowan said after the dress rehearsal. Following a one-week trip to open the regular season, the Giants would return for the official opener with the Los Angeles Dodgers.

Everything But a Win

The day finally arrived when the Giants would move into their new downtown digs for a baseball game that counted, and it was perfect except for the final result. Kevin Elster, who was coaxed out of retirement to be the Dodgers' shortstop, somehow hit three home runs in a 6-5 Opening Day victory, and it really didn't seem to matter.

The Giants had the beautiful ballpark that previous owner Bob Lurie tried so hard to obtain, and 40,930 showed up on a perfect Tuesday afternoon, immediately getting into the spirit by chanting, "Beat L.A! Beat L.A!" prior to pregame ceremonies. Then Kirk Rueter threw the first pitch and Devon White promptly singled for the first hit.

Bill Mueller's single and Barry Bonds's double gave the Giants a quick 1-0 lead off Chan Ho Park in the bottom of the first. After Elster hit the first Pac Bell homer in the third, Bonds answered with a drive to center in the bottom for the Giants' first homer and a 2-1 lead. The Dodgers went ahead to stay on Elster's two-run homer in a three-run fifth.

Elster's third homer came in the eighth inning off Felix Rodriguez. The Giants also hit three homers for a total of six. J. T. Snow and Doug Mirabelli also connected, and the slow-footed Mirabelli legged out the first triple in Pac Bell history and his first in 136 major-league at-bats.

"I liked playing in Candlestick very much, so I miss it because it was one of my favorite places to play," said Elster, who spoiled the Giants' party. "But, obviously, this place isn't too bad, either."

Power to Spare

Barry Bonds went on a record home run spree of his own in 2001. One year earlier, the Giants did as a team, and with better results. At Enron Field, Sept. 11, 2000, Jeff Kent and J. T. Snow hit back-to-back homers off Jose Lima in the first inning, triggering an 8-7 victory over the Houston Astros and setting a San Francisco power standard.

They were the Giants' 205th and 206th homers of the season, erasing the previous S.F. record of 205 by the 1987 division winners. Bonds added a homer in the ninth inning for a total of 207, with 19 games still remaining in the season. They would finish with 226 and another division crown.

"It's like an American League team," GM Brian Sabean said of the distribution of power. Added manager Dusty Baker: "It's better when everyone's doing it." Summed up Kent: "We have a lot of confidence in our offense."

A Perfect Finish

It couldn't have been scripted any better—a beautiful new ballpark, a solid team, a division championship without the normal September stress, and more than three million fans clamoring to get into Pacific Bell Park.

All the components came to a head Sept. 21, 2000, when 40,930 turned out for the clincher on a festive Thursday night. The Giants didn't disappoint. Pinch hitter Russ Davis's eighth-inning sacrifice fly snapped a tie and propelled an 8-7 victory over the Arizona Diamondbacks.

The Giants were champions, and they did it by overcoming a ragged 4-11 start to post their most decisive title run, wrapping it up with 10 games to go and fulfilling the prophecy of GM Brian Sabean and manager Dusty Baker.

"We're not a .500 team," Sabean boldly predicted when the Giants trailed Arizona by nine games with a 22-25 record on May 28. Sure enough, they went 75-40 thereafter to blow the opposition away, including an S.F.-best 59-27 over the final three months.

Baker was even more specific while analyzing his team in spring training, observing: "You always want a good start, but I have a feeling this will be more of a second-half team."

And one whose balance proved decisive. The Giants won the NL West by 11 games without a significant ace, yet five starters had between 11 and 15 victories. And all eight starters and supersub Armando Rios hit at least 10 home runs.

Kent's Consistency Counts

In a situation reminiscent of 1989 when Giants teammates Kevin Mitchell and Will Clark were one-two in the MVP race, strong arguments were made for Barry Bonds and Jeff Kent in 2000. Kent's career batting year (.334) and his season-long consistency prevailed and won with 392 points as compared to Bonds's 279.

"We're not enemies—just different players," Kent said after receiving 22 first-place votes to Bonds's six. "There's no doubt I wouldn't be doing the things I'm doing without him. I've learned a heck of a lot by hitting behind him and watching the way he works pitchers, and I think I complement him very well, too."

Kent, who called the award "overwhelming and surprising," also was the sentimental favorite of many teammates because of his statistical edge over Bonds in most offensive categories, most significantly a 125-106 RBI, a 196-147 hits and a .334-.306 batting average advantage. Bonds outhomered him 49-33.

"Both guys have done one hell of a job, and Barry's had some big homers this month [September], but you've got to look at the whole season," Ellis Burks said. "To me, Jeff is the MVP. It's about being consistent for five or six months, and Jeff has been that."

Added J. T. Snow: "Home runs aren't that big of a deal. Runs batted in are the big stat, and Jeff has been doing the job *all* season. He's been there *every* day. It's Jeff this year."

Perhaps the most poignant endorsement came from Mark McGwire, who hit 70 homers in 1998 and wasn't the MVP. "It's Kent, hands down," Big Mac said. "The MVP isn't about hitting a lot of homers—I learned that in '98."

A Potent Pitcher

Given his penchant for giving up lots of hits and runs, it has often been suggested that Livan Hernandez was a better hitter than a pitcher. On Aug. 11, 2001, at Wrigley Field, the chunky Cuban right-hander demonstrated that notion wasn't so far-fetched.

On a day in which Barry Bonds hit a 50th home run for the first time and Chicago slugger Sammy Sosa also connected, Hernandez grabbed the headlines with four hits, extending his hitting streak to eight in a row in a 9-4 rout of the Cubs.

"I don't know how I do it," said Hernandez, who had 12 hits in 13 at-bats and raised his average to .333. "I was an 18-year-old in Cuba, playing third base. You never forget how to hit. I just look for fastballs."

Hernandez did it against four different pitchers and hit his fourth career home run, a two-run blast to left. The streak fell two shy of the National League record of 10 straight hits by Bip Roberts because Greg Maddux stopped him in the next start.

"I've never seen anything like it," Bonds said of Hernandez's hitting. "He embarrassed all of us. He hit no matter what they threw. It was fun to watch."

Clark...Kent

Barry Bonds wasn't the only Giant setting records in 2001. Teammate Jeff Kent set the franchise mark with 49 doubles, toppling the previous high of 46 by Jack Clark in 1978. In fact, Kent *averaged* 41.2 doubles in six seasons with the club.

"I'm glad it's somebody like him," Clark said of Kent. "He was the MVP [2000] and is a great player. It's not easy to hit that many doubles. I'm proud that I held the record so long, and he's shattered it."

Clark, who also set the franchise record with a 26-game hitting streak in 1978, observed that Kent's doubles record is more legitimate than his was because it was achieved playing home games on grass at Pacific Bell Park.

"I played a lot of games at Candlestick when it had AstroTurf," he recalled. "It was a real fast infield, and I'd turn a lot of chop hits into doubles. The key is staying in the lineup and staying healthy. It's a good record, but hitting doubles isn't a sexy thing."

Dawn Patrol

In perhaps their most unexpected victory of a championship season, the weary Giants somehow pulled off a 5-1 victory over the Milwaukee Brewers on Sept. 20, 2002, pushing their wild-card lead to two games with eight remaining. What made it improbable was the fact it followed a redeye plane flight from Los Angeles.

"No comment on anything, I'm too tired—this whole scenario is a joke," Rich Aurilia said prior to assisting a 5-1 victory with a two-run homer at Miller Park. "I got a burst of energy."

The Giants certainly needed it following an exhausting four-game split in L.A. that consumed 14:04 and an all-night flight. General manager Brian Sabean called it "the turning point," rejuvenating the club in its playoff pursuit.

Kent Comes Through

Jeff Kent was struggling through an 11-for-58 slump that included 20 strikeouts, but he made contact just in time as the Giants concluded the road portion of their 2002 schedule Sept. 22, in Milwaukee with a two-game wild-card lead hanging in the balance.

It was 1-1 in the top of the ninth, and the exhausted Giants didn't need extra innings on a getaway day. Brewers reliever Luis

Vizcaino fired a 1-1 slider that Kent deposited into the left field stands. One out later, Benito Santiago also homered in a 3-1 victory that concluded a 5-2 trip.

"After coming through an emotional series in L.A. and landing here at 6:30 in the morning, it was big that we didn't allow the Brewers to take advantage of us," Kent said after hitting his career-high 37th home run and helping the Giants go 25-14-1 in a string of 40 games in 41 days.

Going Wild

The Giants took a big step by snapping Wade Miller's 12-game winning streak with a 2-1 win in the opener of a final three-game series with the Houston Astros, Sept. 27, and marched into the playoffs the next day when all their components clicked in a 5-2 triumph that clinched the wild card with one day to go.

Jason Schmidt outpitched Miller in the opener, and shutout relief by seven pitchers helped Kirk Rueter win the clincher. Barry Bonds broke a tie with a splash homer into McCovey Cove in the fifth inning and pinch hitter Tom Goodwin added a two-run double in the seventh.

"Been here, done it—seven times," Bonds said above the clubhouse din. "This is nice, but I want to win the World Series."

Champagne-soaked GM Brian Sabean added: "We expected this. There was a silent confidence—it was a matter of time. We stepped up in a lot of big games."

Torrid Twosome

Barry Bonds and Jeff Kent had their share of disagreements, yet they concluded a six-year run as the most consistent one-two punch in San Francisco history, better than any combination that included Hall of Famers Willie Mays, Orlando Cepeda or Willie McCovey.

When Bonds finished 2002 with 46 homers and 110 RBI, and Kent added 37 homers and 108 RBI, their total of 301 marked the ninth time in S.F. that two hitters exceeded 300 homers and RBI. Bonds and Kent accomplished it four times.

The Mays-Cepeda combo registered a club-high 351 in 1961, but they surpassed 300 only one more time. Bonds made the list six of the nine times, joining Rich Aurilia for a 344 total in 2001 and Matt Williams for 317 in 1993.

What Bonds and Kent accomplished as a tandem over six years exceeded what any S.F. teammates did over a comparable stretch. They combined for 454 homers and 1,348 RBI and a 1,802 total. Mays and Cepeda are second best with 1,767 from 1959 to 1964.

Rites Of Spring, from
Casa Grande to Scottsdale

If the Walls Could Talk at
The Pink Pony, Don & Charlie's

Terry's Tour

Bill Terry, the last man to hit .400 in the National League (1930) and a Hall of Fame first baseman, is credited with conceiving the idea of the celebrated Giants-Indians barnstorming tours throughout the U.S. prior to Opening Day.

They originally were known as Terry's Tour, and they were a big hit, bringing major-league baseball to the heartland. The teams travelled by train and were greeted enthusiastically by eager fans in the Southwest, Midwest and South.

"We knew the Indians better than the teams in our league," recalled Bill Rigney. "We'd play them as many as 20 games each spring, and when we got to a town there would be receptions at the train depots and parades down Main Street.

"There was nothing like those trips. We'd break camp in Phoenix, take a train down to Tucson to pick up the Indians, and then wind our way to Cleveland and New York. It was a big deal wherever we went.

"Those trips were fabulous. We used to sleep on the sidings, waiting for the next through train to pick us up. Everyone tried to avoid sleeping in the same car with Ernie Lombardi. He was a great guy, but he snored so loud, it was like an earthquake."

The annual tour began in 1934, and it lasted until 1960. By then, the Giants had moved and it wasn't practical to continue. Eventually, more teams headed west for spring training and it no longer was necessary to exclusively play the Indians.

Prior to the West Coast opener in 1958, the two teams "trained" to El Paso, San Antonio, Austin, Corpus Christi, Harlingen, Houston, Tulsa, Des Moines and Omaha before the Giants headed for Seals Stadium.

As late as 1959, with the opener in St. Louis, the club headed toward Missouri with the Indians by way of Salt Lake City, Denver, Topeka, Des Moines and Omaha. By 1960, the Terry Tour was history.

"It seemed like we played the Indians every day," Herman Franks said. "It was like a playoff atmosphere because they had great pitching and we had the hitting. By the time the season started, we'd faced the best so our hitters were ready."

Stop That Train!

It was the Giants' first season in San Francisco, and Opening Day starter Ruben Gomez's wife was pregnant. She was the nervous type, and the pitcher had sent her ahead to San Francisco while the club was barnstorming through Texas with the Indians.

At about 3:00 a.m., the porter awakened equipment manager Eddie Logan and told him that two State Troopers had stopped the train and wanted to talk to Gomez. It was the middle of a stormy night and the rain was pouring.

"I went over to Ruben's bunk and woke him up," Logan remembered. "We get dressed and the two big Texas State Troopers say that his wife called and that there's an emergency in San Francisco. They sidetracked the train and there's no phone.

"So we've got to go about 10 miles down the road in the State Troopers' car to get to a little public phone. Ruben gets on the phone and calls San Francisco, and he's on the phone five or 10 minutes. And it's really raining.

"He comes out, and I say, 'What's wrong, Ruben? Everything all right?'

"He says, 'Oh, yeah. I was supposed to call my wife before we left, but I forgot to call and she got worried thinking something happened.'

"I asked the Texas Trooper to lend me one of his guns so I could shoot Ruben."

A Clubhouse Lawyer

It was spring training of 1961, and Giants teammates Jim Davenport, Bob Schmidt and newcomer Harvey Kuenn were enjoying a few beers before heading back to their downtown Phoenix digs. About one block from their destination, they come to a stoplight and three men in another auto begin hassling them.

Kuenn was driving, and Schmidt, sitting in the passenger seat, said something to one of the strangers, who proceeded to get out of the car. He was joined by his two friends, so Davenport also stepped onto the street. Kuenn told his buddies he was going to park the car and be right back.

"Then it's me and Schmitty, three of them and a buddy of theirs who shows up," Davenport recalled. "The friend claims Schmitty hit him, and someone said something about calling the cops. Before you know it, a squad car shows up, and the cops take us by the arm and pull us in.

"While this is going on, Harvey shows up and the cop asks him, 'Who are you?' Harvey says, 'I'm Davenport's lawyer,' and they pull him in, too. I'll never forget that look on Harv's face.

"It was a memorable experience because they threw us in the tank with a lot of drunks and derelicts. We were in there for a couple of hours until [manager] Alvin Dark and [traveling secretary] Eddie Brannick came and got us out. And Alvin, who didn't drink, didn't hold it against us."

Sad Sam's Lament

When Alvin Dark took over as manager in 1961, he didn't endear himself to the pitchers because he believed in working them hard and having a lot of running drills. This especially perturbed Stu Miller and Sam Jones.

"One day, Sad Sam really had it," catcher Tom Haller recalled. "He ran up to Dark, huffing and puffing, and said, 'Geezus, Skip, you can't run the ball across the plate!' Everyone cracked up."

The Real First Game

The Giants played their first game in San Francisco uniforms March 8, 1958, in Tucson against their longtime spring training partner, the Cleveland Indians, winning 5-1. Mike McCormick, then 19, fired three scoreless innings for the victory.

Rookie first baseman Orlando Cepeda, 20, described by manager Bill Rigney as looking "like a bronze statue standing at dress parade," broke in with a homer, a double, a single and three RBI.

The next day, the Giants played their home exhibition opener in Phoenix and prevailed by an identical 5-1 score against the Chicago Cubs. Rookie Joe Shipley and Al Worthington each threw three scoreless innings.

Passing the Test

Will "The Thrill" Clark was a high first-round draft choice, but that didn't exempt him from some rookie hazing when he arrived in Arizona for spring training in 1986. A group of playful veterans tested Clark's sense of humor early, and he passed.

It was March 13, his birthday, so Clark entered the clubhouse in a good mood following a workout. Then he peered into his locker and was stunned to find his prized lizard cowboy boots spray-painted a bright orange and with the inscription Air Thrill.

"All I could do was laugh," Clark recalled. "It caught me completely by surprise, but I knew they'd test me. I really wasn't too happy about it because they were a great pair of boots, and expensive, too."

Clark's teammates quickly discovered the star rookie could take a joke, so they made amends for his indoctrination. They passed the hat, and the very next day a brand-new pair of lizard boots were in Will's locker when he arrived.

"Will handled it pretty well," teammate Mike Krukow said, "but he wasn't all that happy with the replacement boots. They cost us $250, but Will told me his old pair had sentimental value, a gift for being on the Olympic team."

A Real Fowl Ball

For a player with limited playing time, Calvin Murray had a knack for getting in on the action during a bizarre 2001 season. It all started in a spring training game against the Arizona Diamondbacks in Tucson, where Murray was at bat against Randy Johnson in the seventh inning.

This time, Johnson didn't do any serious damage to the Giants, but a 95-mph fastball to Murray struck a dove in flight and killed it instantly. The Big Unit was unnerved, and after Jeff Kent picked up the dead bird and removed it, Murray doubled on the next pitch.

"Seeing a bird killed like that is unbelievable," Kent said. "I should ask Randy to come to the ranch to hunt. He can bring a bucket of balls instead of a shotgun. If you put a bird on a stick and gave him 100 chances to hit it, he couldn't do it."

Others were equally amazed. "I've never seen that before, and I'll never see it again," Diamondbacks catcher Rod Barajas said. "That ball was three-quarters of the way to plate. It was an explosion of feathers."

Added Murray: "The ball was three feet from the plate, and it just disappeared. It exploded. Nothing but feathers everywhere. Just poof."

Kent's Negative Spin

Jeff Kent's falling-out with Giants management, one that ended with his departure as a free agent at the end of the season, was never more apparent than in spring training 2002. He insisted that his broken wrist was the result of slipping while washing his truck, instead of owning up to the fact that it happened when he spun out of control and fell off his motorbike.

The brass got even over the embarrassing lie by hitting Kent where it hurt him most. They wouldn't let him play after the highly motivated infielder worked hard to be ready by Opening Day. General manager Brian Sabean kept him on the disabled list for the first four games, and Kent expressed his displeasure.

"Too bad for Jeff—I'm up to here with Jeff," Sabean snapped. "He should have thought more about his actions that put him and the club in this position. I didn't break his wrist. What I say is 'Tough luck,' quote, unquote."

But unlike pitcher Ron Bryant, whose career was shortened by a spring training swimming pool mishap in 1974, the driven Kent rebounded with one of his finest seasons, getting a last laugh along with a contract from the Houston Astros after batting .313 with 108 RBI and a career-high 37 home runs.

Giants-Dodgers:
The Rivalry Moves West

Playoff Shocker,
Marichal vs. Roseboro Continued Tradition

Zimmer Goes Ballistic

It was one of the early Giants-Dodgers games at the L.A. Coliseum, and Willie Mays hit a shot down the line and off the high left field screen. Umpire Dusty Boggess signaled a home run, and Dodgers shortstop Don Zimmer was quick to protest.

"Boggess changes his mind and calls it a ground-rule double, and here come the Giants to argue," Don Drysdale recalled. "Now all of us are out there, yelling and screaming. All of a sudden, all the arguing stops.

"Zimmer always had this big chaw of tobacco in his mouth, and he was yelling so hard, the chaw came out and his [dental] plate came with it. Everyone stopped arguing and started looking for Zimmer's plate."

Bombs Away

Giants-Dodgers games usually were characterized either by great L.A. pitching or by prodigious S.F. slugging. The latter definitely was the case May 13, 1958, at the Coliseum, where the Giants set a major-league record with 50 total bases in a 26-hit 16-9 rout.

Willie Mays, as usual, led the way with five hits in five at-bats, totaling 15 bases on two homers, two triples and a single as the Giants pounced on starter Don Newcombe and four relievers, including Sandy Koufax.

Mays had lots of help. In something that's probably never been done, Orlando Cepeda, Darryl Spencer, Bob Schmidt and Danny O'Connell—the Nos. 5-8 hitters—each had four hits. Spencer had two homers and a double, driving in six runs. Mays had four RBI.

The Giants gave a hint of what was to come the previous day, pounding the Dodgers 12-3 with 17 hits. Mays had three hits and five RBI in that one. He and Spencer each hit two home runs, giving them four in the two games. This time, it was Don Drysdale who was routed.

A Real Labor Day

During the Seals-Oaks rivalry in the Pacific Coast League, there occasionally would be Sunday doubleheaders with one game being played in San Francisco and the other in Oakland. The Giants didn't carry it to that extreme, but there was a unique day-night twin bill on Labor Day in 1958.

Ostensibly "for the convenience of the public" at undersized Seals Stadium, the first game was scheduled for 10:00 a.m., after which the ballpark was emptied before fans were readmitted for the 2:30 matinee. A total of 33,921 watched the doubleheader, and the Dodgers were grumbling following two defeats and nearly 12 hours at the ballpark.

San Francisco police chief Frank Ahern died of a heart attack during the 15th inning of the second game. The Giants won it in the 16th on Ray Jablonski's bunt single and throwing errors by catcher John Roseboro and right fielder Carl Furillo, ending a game that consumed four hours and 35 minutes.

The long doubleheader was part of a rare six-game series between the clubs. The Dodgers won the opener, but the Giants took the next five behind the blazing bat of Willie Mays, who had seven straight hits at one juncture. He finished the series with 11 hits and 27 total bases in 20 at-bats, bashing four homers, two doubles and a triple.

A Fog Delay

A lot of strange things happen when the Giants engage the Dodgers, and July 15, 1960, was no exception. It was so foggy at Candlestick Park that umpire Frank Dascoli waved the players off the field and delayed the game 24 minutes. That hadn't happened in San Francisco in 40 years, since a Pacific Coast League fogout at Ewing Field.

When the thick mist shrouded Candlestick, it obscured the scoreboard and a towering drive by Willie McCovey fell for a triple in left center when outfielders Wally Moon and Duke Snider couldn't see it. That's when Dascoli decided to clear the field. When play resumed, the Dodgers posted a 5-3 victory.

"It was like a scene from the early days on earth," remarked Dodgers coach Bobby Bragan. "You expected cavemen, dressed in animal skins and bearing clubs, to appear through the mist, followed by dinosaurs and other prehistoric monsters.

"But," he added, "actually, nothing emerged except Wally Moon, Duke Snider and Willie Mays—and all were quite clean-shaven."

The Swamp Fox

Maury Wills swiped a record 104 bases and nudged Willie Mays for MVP honors in 1962, but at least the Giants had the satisfaction of winning the pennant and aggravating the Dodgers with Matty Schwab's handiwork prior to the opener of a crucial series at Candlestick. The groundskeeper explained:

"At 5:30 in the morning, so nobody would see us, we took two bales of peat moss, with sand and topsoil, and laid it by first base, about five feet wide and 15 feet long. It was loose, and I knew they would squawk.

"When the Dodgers saw it, they started kicking the dirt. [Coach] Leo Durocher got on his knees and said, 'What the hell is going on?' He's digging down about six inches, and he still hasn't hit bottom."

The Dodgers protested to umpire Jocko Conlan and threatened to forfeit the game. Schwab's crew then filled three wheelbarrows with the soft soil and rolled them away. Schwab then instructed his son "to make a lake out of the first base area."

Now it looked like a swamp, and the Dodgers were making duck calls. First baseman Ron Fairly asked Giants manager Alvin Dark, "What time does the tide come in?"

So Conlon had Schwab bring the loaded wheelbarrows back to first base and covered the water with the original peat moss mixture.

"It was looser than before, but it satisfied the umps," Schwab said. "Then Willie Davis came around first on a hit, slipped and was thrown out. Wills tried to steal and was thrown out by 20 feet. He called the ump a name and got thrown out."

Many years later, when asked if there really was that much water, Wills dryly replied: "I still have a cold from that day. The grounds crew was standing in one spot with no nozzles on the hoses for three or four minutes."

It came as no surprise when the Giants players, appreciative of Schwab's gardening skills, offered him a full World Series share.

Wait Till Next Year

New Giants manager Felipe Alou was a key player on the 1962 champions, enjoying his finest year with the club by batting .316 with 25 home runs and a career-high 98 RBI. He also made a game-winning catch to steal extra bases from Tommy Davis in a game with the Dodgers that season, a diving grab he regards as his best fielding play ever.

"When we were down [4-2] in the ninth inning of the final playoff game, I would not admit that we were going to lose," he thought to himself before the Giants rallied to win the pennant.

"We saw the Dodgers in St. Louis about one month before the end of the season, and they were saying things like, 'We'll see you next year.' And then they had to see us again. That was quite an experience to beat them."

Sad Sam's Saddest Day

It was June 30, 1959, at the Los Angeles Coliseum, and Giants ace Sam Jones carried a no-hitter into the eighth inning. Then Jim Gilliam hit what seemed like a routine grounder to erratic S.F. shortstop Andre Rodgers, who fielded the ball, dropped it, and didn't make a throw.

Official scorer Charlie Park of the *Los Angeles Mirror-News*, a grizzled baseball writer, immediately called it a hit. The Giants were infuriated, Jones sulked, and Park refused to change the call despite protests from many of his press box colleagues who adhered to the adage that the first hit must be clean.

"If ever a man deserved a no-hit game, Sam Jones did tonight—the ball was a routine grounder," Giants announcer Russ Hodges complained on the air.

Added a tearful Jones: "Man, I guess they just don't want no-hitters thrown here. Imagine anybody calling that one a hit!"

Antonelli's Downfall

Left-hander Johnny Antonelli was a successful starter for the Giants, but he fell victim to the wind at Seals Stadium on July 20, 1959, and it was the beginning of the end of his career in San Francisco. During a day game against the Dodgers, Gil Hodges's two-run homer in the first inning and Charley Neal's wind-aided blast in the ninth gave the visitors a 3-2 victory.

Afterward, a reporter asked Antonelli what kind of pitch Neal hit for the game-winning blow, and the pitcher temporarily lost his cool in the first major complaint about the climate in San Francisco.

"What difference does it make what kind of pitch I threw?" an agitated Antonelli snapped. "I was beat by two lousy fly balls. A pitcher should be paid double for working here. It's the worst ballpark in America. Every time you stand out there, you've got to beat the hitter and a 30-mph wind. This park is a disgrace."

Antonelli's comments, of course, made headlines, and he immediately became Public Enemy No. 1 for having the audacity to assail San Francisco's cooling breezes. Editorials suggested that he return to New York, and the pummeled pitcher refused to speak with the press the remainder of the season, further fueling the discontent.

Whatever the reason, Antonelli was 14-5 at the time of the incident and the Giants were in first place. He won only five more games in the remaining 11 weeks of the season, and the club dropped out of the race down the stretch. One year later, Antonelli was traded (along with Willie Kirkland) to the Cleveland Indians for Harvey Kuenn.

"The score was tied, and Neal hit a fly ball," Antonelli recalled several years later. "Daryl Spencer is the shortstop, and he calls for it. Then Jackie Brandt comes in from left field, and he says he's got it. And now, all of a sudden, Brandt looks up and the ball blows out of the ballpark."

Antonelli also conceded that he may have overreacted to the criticism, adding: "I felt a little sorry for myself. After that, I never pitched another ballgame effectively. I think it took just enough wind out of my sails where I felt the press and the fans were coming down a little too hard on me."

A former two-time 20-game winner for the Giants, Antonelli was so bitter over the repercussions that followed his flareup that he turned down an opportunity to pitch the final game of the season in a bid for his 20th victory. He also asked for a trade and was accommodated by general manager Chub Feeney.

The Roseboro Incident

It was Aug. 22, 1965, a sunny Sunday afternoon at Candlestick Park, when the ugliest confrontation in the Giants-Dodgers West Coast rivalry erupted. It was triggered when Maury Wills faked a bunt and was awarded first base on catcher Tom Haller's interference in the series opener Friday night.

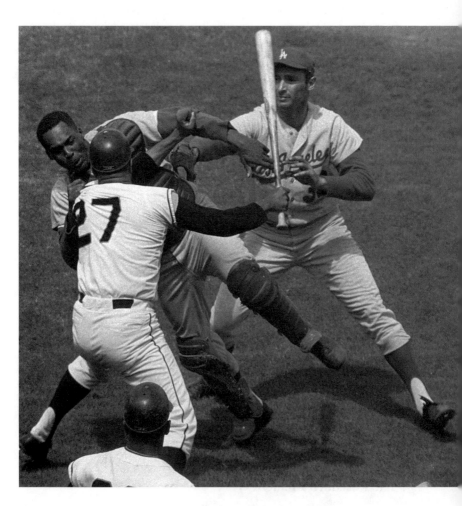

*Juan Marichal (27) goes after John Roseboro with a bat after
Roseboro's return throw to pitcher Sandy Koufax (right) almost hit
Marichal. Koufax attempts to break it up. (AP/WWP)*

When the Giants batted, Matty Alou was instructed to do likewise, but when his bat struck catcher John Roseboro's glove, he wasn't awarded first base, and the jawing ensued. Roseboro began threatening the Giants, and Marichal yelled from the dugout, reminding the catcher that Wills had done the same thing. Roseboro then reportedly cracked: "Tell Juan to shut his big mouth before he gets one behind his ear."

Emotions ebbed until it was Marichal's turn to pitch against Sandy Koufax before 42,807 in the series finale. Wills led off with a bunt single, stole second and scored on Ron Fairly's double for a 1-0 lead. When Wills batted the second time, it was 2-0, and Marichal elected to pitch him inside, dissuading a bunt.

Marichal's pitch knocked Wills out of the box, and the Dodgers' dugout began acting up. Fairly also hit the deck, adding fuel to the fire when the Giants' ace went to the plate in the bottom of the third.

"I took the first pitch for a ball," Marichal recalled, "and the second one was right over the plate for a strike. When I looked back, I saw Roseboro drop it behind me. When he threw it back to Sandy, the ball ticked my ear and I got goose pimples all over my body.

"I knew if that ball had hit me square, it could have killed me. I never expected him throwing the ball like that. I asked him why he did it, and I really got angry when he started talking about my mother, calling her all kinds of names.

"I asked him once again, and he gave me the same answer, and then he made the first move. He started coming at me, and my first reaction was to stop him. If I wanted to hurt him bad, I could have done it. But I just dropped the bat on his head, trying to stop him."

Marichal regretted using the bat, opening a wound that required stitches, but insisted it was in self-defense. Tito Fuentes and Orlando Cepeda also had bats held high, but struck nobody. Marichal was fined a record $1,750 and suspended for nine games.

"I thought it had knocked Roseboro's eye out," Dodgers manager Walter Alston said. "There was nothing but blood where his left eye should have been. A man might as well have a gun as use a bat like that."

Roseboro filed charges, and it was settled out of court when Marichal paid him $7,500. The two didn't speak for years, but settled their differences as Dodger teammates in1975.

The Giants, with the help of Willie Mays's three-run homer off Koufax when order was restored in the bottom of the third, won the game 4-3, had a 14-game winning streak and a four and one-half-game lead in mid-September, but faded at the finish as the Dodgers won the pennant.

The Devil Made Him Do It

Juan Marichal, of course, wasn't blameless. Matty Alou remembered his good friend and roommate being especially agitated that entire weekend series. Maury Wills's bunt and Ron Fairly's double were the last straw that fateful Sunday.

"After the first inning," Alou recalled, "Juan came into the dugout, threw his glove down and said, 'I'm going to kill those guys—we've got to win and I've got to get him [Wills] out of here, and I'm going to get Fairly, too.'

"So, here comes Wills the next time, and he threw four times right at his legs. Wills was jumping all over. He walked him, and then he hit Fairly real good. Then when Juan's time to bat came, Johnny Roseboro wanted Sandy Koufax to hit him.

"But Koufax didn't want to do it. Roseboro saw that Koufax wasn't going to hit him, so he threw the ball back right next to Juan's head. So Juan turned around and hit him. Juan wanted to fight all day. He had the devil inside him that day.

"When Juan and Roseboro were fighting, we had to go out there, too. They had about 10 guys on top of him, and I saw Bob Miller trying to break his leg, so I had to hit the guy because he was twisting Juan's leg."

What Fight?

Don Drysdale, who was involved in a lot of confrontations with the Giants and was known for frequently buzzing Willie Mays, missed the Marichal-Roseboro fracas because he was on an airplane heading for New York, where he was to pitch the next day.

"I sat in first class, relaxing and having a nice martini," Drysdale said. "When I got off the plane, a bunch of reporters came running up and asked what I thought of the fight?

"I said there was no fight in first class—it must have been in coach."

Dietz, Drysdale and Wendelstedt

It was May 31, 1968, and the first-place Giants were at Dodger Stadium, where Don Drysdale was going for a record-tying five consecutive shutouts. The bases were loaded with no outs in the top of the ninth inning and the count was 2-2 on Dick Dietz.

"He threw a spitball, I was protecting the plate and he hit me on the elbow," Dietz explained. "All I had time to do was flinch. I took two steps toward first base and [plate umpire Harry] Wendelstedt says, 'No!'

"And I said, 'No, what?'

"He said, 'No, you didn't try to get out of the way.'

"I was hot. It was the worst call, without a doubt, that I've ever seen. I didn't try to get hit with the ball. I really never gave any thought to breaking Drysdale's streak. I was guarding the plate, trying to make contact."

Wendelstedt's generosity enabled Drysdale to complete a six-hit, 3-0 shutout, extending his streak. In his next start, Dandy Don made it six shutouts in a row, breaking the major-league record—with an assist from a generous umpire who was wrong in taking the streak into account.

"A gutsy call," remarked Dodgers catcher Jeff Torborg.

Resounded Giants GM Chub Feeney: "It would have been gutsy if he had made it in San Francisco."

The Great Arrival

Throughout his minor-league career, Bobby Bonds was billed as "the next Willie Mays," because he had speed, power and a flair for playing the game. A marvelous athlete, Bobby was batting .370 for Triple-A Fresno when he was summoned to play his first major-league game, June 25, 1968, against the Dodgers at Candlestick Park.

As the game progressed, reliever John Purdin was pitching for L.A. when Willie Mays led off an inning with a bunt single and Willie McCovey and Jim Ray Hart walked, loading the bases. After Jack Hiatt struck out, Bonds went to the plate for his third big-league at-bat and homered off a Purdin fastball.

"I had seen Purdin in the minors, so I kind of had an idea how he threw and how hard he threw," recalled Bonds, the first player since 1898 to hit a grand slam in his first major-league game. "I told myself, 'If he throws me a fastball, don't miss it.' He wound up and threw a fastball, and I hit it hard.

"When I was called up, I hadn't slept the whole night in Phoenix. Herman Franks, the manager, asked me if I wanted to play, and I said no at first because I was dead tired. Then I thought more about it, and figured I was in the big leagues, so I might as well play. I batted seventh and it was a tremendous thrill to play in front of 40,000 people."

And That Goes for Me, Too

Dick Dietz recalled a particularly volatile series between the Giants and the Dodgers in 1971, when the two clubs finished one-two in the National League West. Juan Marichal was pitching and Maury Wills was the batter. The fact that both were well past their prime didn't lessen the intensity.

"Bill Singer hit Willie Mays with a pitch," Dietz remembered, "and Juan tried to hit Wills in the knee three times. Wills finally made an out, and the next batter was Bill Buckner, so Juan buried one right in his ribs.

"Buckner walked toward the mound with his bat. When Buckner finally went to first base, Gaylord Perry went over to him and said, 'You think he hit you? I'm pitching tomorrow night, and I'm really going to drill you.'

"That's how it was back then. They'd throw at us, and we'd throw at them. We'd take guys out at second base a little harder against the Dodgers."

Fox Hunts Lasorda

One of the best fights involving the Giants and the Dodgers didn't include players. It was between Giants manager Charlie Fox and Dodgers third base coach Tommy Lasorda near the batting cage in 1973, and it was triggered when Fox took exception at Lasorda yelling at the S.F. pitchers from the coaching box.

"I told him to cut it out, and one thing led to another," Fox recalled. "He mouthed off and I told him to come and get me. He threw a punch and it missed, hitting my arm. I wouldn't retaliate because I was a [karate] black belt. He said he wanted me to kick, so he could grab my leg and twist it."

Lasorda, of course, has a slightly different version: "The night before the national TV game we had a head-hunting contest. Guys were throwing at each other. Elias Sosa was pitching for the Giants, and I was screaming at him from third base. The next morning, Fox tells me not to yell at his pitcher.

"I told him, 'I don't care what you want—I'll holler at him any time I want.' He said, 'No you won't,' and I said, 'Well, who's going to stop me?' He said, 'Me,' and I said, 'Go ahead.'

"Charlie used to tell me he's a black belt, so I'm waiting for his leg to come up because I wanted to upend him when he lifted his leg. But he didn't do it. The guy's no black belt, so we started fighting. When we were being separated, I stepped on [Giants coach] Joey Amalfitano's foot, tore up his shoe and had to get him a new pair."

A One-Sided Hiring Policy

The number of players who wore both Giants' and Dodgers' uniforms reached 48 when Marquis Grissom was signed as a free agent for 2003. It's an illustrious list, one that includes Hall of Famers Juan Marichal and Duke Snider.

But it doesn't carry over into the managing ranks, where the Giants have seemed eager to tap former Dodgers for leadership roles, but the favor hasn't been returned by Los Angeles management.

The three winningest managers in San Francisco history are former Dodgers Dusty Baker (840), Roger Craig (586), and Herman Franks (387), all of whom played for L.A., as did Clyde King (109) and Frank Robinson (264).

And longtime Dodgers coach Danny Ozark served as the Giants' interim skipper in 1984 after Robinson was fired. Ex-Dodgers pitching coach Ron Perranoski also served in that capacity with San Francisco.

The Count Fuels the Flames

John Montefusco hated the Dodgers as a New Jersey youngster because they blitzed his Yankees in the 1963 World Series. But the intensity of that hatred didn't surface until he became immersed in the Giants-Dodgers rivalry.

It happened immediately. In his major-league debut, not long after he donned his uniform for the first time, Montefusco was thrust into a bases-loaded, no-outs situation in the first inning at Dodger Stadium.

"I couldn't believe it," he said. "When [manager] Wes Westrum told me I'd be the first reliever, I had all kinds of butterflies. I didn't know who was batting for the Dodgers. I didn't know their names. I just threw the ball."

He proceeded to work nine innings, yielding one run and hitting a home run in his first major-league victory. He also became a thorn in the side of the Dodgers, who resented his boasts and trash talk, part of the Montefusco mystique.

"I really didn't think there was that much rivalry between the Giants and the Dodgers until I joined the Giants," he said. "I could actually feel the rivalry right there. I'd say a few things about the Dodgers, and they'd say things about me.

"I went on radio in San Francisco in 1975 and said, 'Watch me tonight—I'm pitching against the Dodgers and I'm going to shut them out.' I did it because Ron Cey said a couple of things like I wouldn't win 10 games in the big leagues.

"So we went down to Dodger Stadium and I went on television and said the same thing, that I was going to shut them out. Well, I beat them 1-0 that night and I got all over Cey, and it worked out pretty good. I started making predictions."

Montefusco vs. Smith

Among all the Dodgers that John Montefusco antagonized over the years, none was as agitated as Reggie Smith. The intense L.A. outfielder was in a constant war of words with the cocky pitcher, and whereas The Count usually was kidding, Smith wasn't laughing.

"I struck him out five times in a row once, so he started leaving messages for me on the mound, stuff like band-aids for my blisters and little notes that were antagonistic," Montefusco said before the feud escalated when the Giants once again became contenders in 1978.

Smith that season: "He's a liar and a braggart. I don't like him. He keeps popping off about what he's going to do to us, but he hasn't done it yet. Most of the guys we face are professionals, but he demeans his profession.

"I'll do anything in my power to beat him, and I mean anything. And they'll [Giants] never finish ahead of us. I'll never concede a thing to them until I see a flag hanging on that pole. They're lucky, that's what they are."

An amused Montefusco retorted: "Lucky? Hey, that's the way they always beat us, with a bunch of cheap hits. A lot of guys here hate the Dodgers. You hear a lot of guys saying they don't care who wins the pennant, as long as it's not L.A."

Dodgers manager Tommy Lasorda joined the verbal fray with: "Montefusco leads a charmed life. I'd like to buy him for what I think he's worth, and then sell him for what he thinks he's worth. I'd make a million dollars."

Up Close and Personal

Reggie Smith didn't like the Giants or their fans, as was clearly evident during a late 1970s game at Candlestick Park. An elderly peanut vendor was at work near the Dodgers' dugout. Smith spotted him and thought he'd have some fun with manager Tommy Lasorda.

"Didn't you once play baseball with Lasorda?" Smith shouted at the 80-something vendor, who didn't grasp the humor. But Smith persisted, and some young fans started getting on him verbally.

Well, tempers flared and more fans joined in the taunting. One who had a little too much to drink got up the courage to invite the feisty Dodger into the stands, to which Smith replied:

"I can't come up—why don't you come down here? Then we'll settle it." The jawing continued, and the rowdy fan challenged Smith with: "What will it take to get you up here? What if I take off this helmet and throw it at you?"

When Smith replied, "That just might do it," the unruly fan took off his plastic batting helmet and flung it, striking the player on the hip. Without hesitation, Smith was in the stands, and was soon joined by teammates Davey Lopes and Jay Johnstone.

Security guards got to the fan before Smith could reach him, but it took a while to restore order. Smith was fined $5,000 by the National League and sued for $5 million by the fan, who claimed he had a broken hand and fractured ribs.

"Reggie was a raw nerve," Bob Brenly recalled. "You were never quite sure what was going to happen. He was a no-nonsense guy who didn't take any bull from opponents or from his teammates. He wasn't afraid to speak if he was in a situation that needed to be corrected."

Just ask the fans at Candlestick Park.

The Sucker Got Punched

It was February 17, 1979, just before Jim Lefebvre left his coaching position with the Dodgers to take a similar job with the Giants. But not before there was some unfinished business with Tommy Lasorda. Lefebvre, fired by the Dodgers after the 1978 season, reported to Casa Grande, Ariz., intending to keep mum on his feud with the manager.

But Lefebvre was angered by a report that he had sucker-punched Lasorda and gave his version of the altercation which occurred at a Burbank TV studio, where he and the manager were to tape shows at different times, Feb. 17.

"Tommy said it was a sucker punch—well, it was the sucker who got punched, all right," Lefebvre said, recounting the incident and pointing out that Lasorda waited for him at the station when his taping was done and attacked him verbally.

"He used an obscenity and told me I was disloyal to him and to the Dodgers, and that he'd given me the opportunity of a lifetime and that I blew it. I told him, 'You can't talk to me like that any more. I don't work for you any more, and I don't have to take it.'

"Then he took off his coat and cocked his arm, and I decked him. His lip was bleeding, and it definitely wasn't bleeding Dodger blue. He kept saying, 'Look what you've done to me—I'll sue.'

"I tried all winter to avoid a confrontation. The studio assured me Tommy would be gone when I got there. But he was still there, so I went into a room by myself. But when he came looking for me, I knew I couldn't hide from him the rest of my life."

The Dodger Killer

The Dodgers should have known it could happen. It was the final day of the 1982 season, and they needed a win at Candlestick Park to defend their pennant. But it was October 3, a date that will live in infamy for the Dodgers, a date on which Bobby Thomson's homer knocked them out in 1951, and a date on which they lost the deciding playoff game in 1962.

Deja vu, indeed. It was 2-2 in the bottom of the seventh, and Tom Niedenfuer took over for FernandoValenzuela. Rookie catcher Bob Brenly, leading off, singled to center. Pinch hitter Champ Summers doubled off the fence in right, sending Brenly to third.

With no effective pitchers remaining, manager Frank Robinson allowed Greg Minton to bat, and he struck out. Terry Forster then struck out pinch hitter Jim Wohlford, bringing long-time Dodgers nemesis Joe Morgan to the plate.

Ahead of Morgan 1-2, Forster attempted a slider low and away. Instead, it headed straight over the plate and Morgan hammered it into the right field stands at Candlestick Park, powering a 5-3 victory before 47,457 delirious Giants partisans. The Atlanta Braves were beaten 5-1 in San Diego, and it didn't matter.

They were the champions by one game, and the Dodgers were heartbroken—again—on October 3. A September slump by the Braves enabled the Giants and Dodgers to get back in the race. The Giants, nine games behind on Sept. 1, finished third, two games out.

Eliminating the Dodgers made it more bearable. Morgan showed rare emotion by thrusting his hands upward while circling the bases. It was instant redemption because the Dodgers had eliminated the Giants with a 15-4 clubbing the previous day.

"I wanted this one for the Giants and the fans," Morgan said. "I've hit some pretty meaningful home runs, but that one was right up there. It meant so much for the Giants and their fans to beat the Dodgers that day."

Cey, Garvey Targets

Most of the boos when the Dodgers visited Candlestick Park were reserved for manager Tommy Lasorda, but players like Ron Cey, Steve Garvey and Reggie Smith all were targets, and for different reasons.

Cey was booed because he was a Giant-killer, smacking 24 homers at The Stick. Only Dale Murphy and Willie Stargell, with 25, hit more among visitors. Smith got it because of his temper, once going after a heckler in the stands. Garvey was disliked for his goody-goody Hollywood image.

"I loved going there for that alone," Cey said. "We were a big rival, and they loved to boo us. They loved picking on me because I had big success there. I had people yelling at me as soon as I walked out of the tunnel. I had them calling me anything and everything."

Garvey: "I remember walking back to the tunnel after a one-run loss, and something whizzed by me. It was a gin bottle. I picked it up and saw it was half full. Right then, you knew you were at Candlestick. In New York, they would have kept it full for more impact. At Candlestick, they had to drink half of it to keep warm."

Rivals and Teammates

When free agent Marquis Grissom signed with the Giants prior to the 2003 season, the veteran outfielder became the 48th player to wear the uniform of each team since they moved to California in 1958, not counting coaches and managers.

That's nearly one per each of their 46 seasons on the West Coast, but it took a while for the ill feelings to subside following Horace Stoneham's acquisition of Jackie Robinson in December of 1956—only to have Robinson retire rather than join the Giants.

In fact, it took more than 11 years for the archrivals to consummate a significant deal, that coming on Feb. 13, 1968, when the Giants traded catcher Tom Haller to Los Angeles for infielders Ron Hunt and Nate Oliver near the start of spring training.

A Fantasy Camp

It was Fan Appreciation Day in the Giants' final home game of the 1986 season, but it resembled a spring training opener. A total of 52 players were used, one shy of the major-league record, and the depleted rosters had players out of position as the Giants staggered to a 6-5 victory in 16 innings.

There have been many bizarre ballgames in Giants-Dodgers lore, and this one surely ranked with the best, or worst of them, depending on one's point of view. Dodgers manager Tommy Lasorda called it a nightmare and was in a sour mood after closer Greg Minton's double and Bob Brenly's single concluded a five-hour, 45-minute marathon.

Running out of players, manager Roger Craig finished the game with pitcher Jeff Robinson in right field, outfielder Candy Maldonado at third base, outfielder Joel Youngblood at shortstop and first baseman Harry Spilman at second. Craig also used two pitchers as pinch hitters and played pitcher Randy Bockus in right field for one inning.

"It was a Fantasy Camp infield," said Minton, who had his first two hits of the season. "When a ball was hit, I was afraid to turn around."

Lasorda was livid when a reporter suggested it was a great game, snapping: "I don't give a damn how great it was. It's not great when a pitcher hits a double to beat you. This was a nightmare. They had pitchers in the outfield for three innings, and not one guy could hit a ball to them. I'm tired of it."

Of course, Lasorda's anguish added to the Giants' pleasure, as Brenly summed up: "I guess that's the real highlight of the game—Lasorda's so ticked off, he can't eat."

Down but Not Out

The Giants' 1989 pennant push was fueled by some amazing comebacks and contributions from unexpected sources down the stretch. The final home series with the Dodgers was a vivid example of both.

On Sept. 19, Giant-killer Orel Hershiser had a 2-0 lead in the fifth inning when the Giants loaded the bases with two outs. Craig lifted Matt Williams for pinch hitter Mike Laga, and the career minor leaguer belted a three-run double for a 3-2 victory. That was nothing compared to what happened the next night.

The Giants fell behind 7-0 after three innings, but Ernest Riles's two-run homer helped to cut the deficit to 7-3 entering the bottom of the ninth, where Jay Howell retired the first two batters. Many of 21,420 were headed for the parking lot when a miracle unfolded.

"This is the best one I've ever seen—unbelievable," Mike Krukow declared after the Giants somehow emerged with an 8-7 victory that maintained their four and one-half-game lead with 10 games remaining. "The rivalry with the Dodgers is as old as the hills, and this just makes it better."

Kevin Mitchell started the rally with a 420-foot homer to center for 7-4. Riles singled and scored on Williams's double for 7-5. Terry Kennedy's double cut the lead to one run, and Mike Benjamin ran for him. Mike Hartley replaced Howell and pinch hitter Chris Speier's double placed both runners in scoring position.

Pinch hitter Greg Litton knocked in the tying run with a single, sending Speier to third. Brett Butler then lined a single down the right field line, ending the game.

Trevor the Terrible

The 1991 Dodgers were in first place for 134 days, ahead by nine and one-half-games at the All-Star break, and held a one-game lead over the Atlanta Braves with four games remaining.

Darren Lewis singled, and Robby Thompson homered off Greg Hansell for 3-3. Then Barry Bonds singled and scored on Matt Williams's double, ending the five-hour, 16-minute classic with a 4-3 victory.

"You could have easily just sat there after they dropped a three-spot on us, but there really was no letdown," Thompson said. Concluded Dusty Baker: "That ranks at the top, the best. We just kept saying it's not over till we say it's over. I'm sure the guys are tired, but they'd be a lot more tired if we had lost."

Johnson's Finest Hour

The weary Giants had just lost four in a row on a trip to Atlanta and Florida, returning home two games behind the Dodgers, who could have pulled away in a two-game series at Candlestick Park, Sept. 17-18.

For openers, Darryl Hamilton's one-out walk and Barry Bonds's homer off Chan Ho Park gave the Giants a 2-0 lead that Kirk Rueter and Roberto Hernandez protected for a 2-1 victory before 50,921.

That cut the Dodgers' lead to one game and set the stage for more tension the following night, when 52,140 gathered in perhaps the Giants' most important game of the season. They weren't disappointed.

J. T. Snow's fourth-inning homer snapped a 1-1 tie, and the Giants added three runs in the fifth on singles by Hamilton and Bill Mueller followed by Bonds's homer off Tom Candiotti. That 5-1 lead soon evaporated when the Dodgers scored twice in the sixth and pulled into a tie on Mike Piazza's two-run single in the seventh.

It stayed that way, with Rod Beck surviving a scare and working three extra innings. With a division tie hanging in the balance, catcher Brian Johnson became an unlikely hero for the Giants. He led off the bottom of the 12th by sending a Mark Guthrie first pitch over the left field fence for a dramatic walk-off homer and a first-place tie.

"It was a lot of fun—this makes it interesting," said Bonds, who rushed to the plate and bowed toward Johnson. The catcher also enjoyed it after providing one of the most thrilling moments in Giants history, adding: "I've never hit a bigger homer—it was important for us to win the two games, and we did."

But not before Beck provided an anxious moment when the Dodgers loaded the bases with no outs in the 10th. "I had to find a way to get out of it," said Beck, who retired Todd Zeile on a called third strike and induced pinch hitter Eddie Murray into hitting into an inning-ending double play.

The Check Will Be Late

The Dodgers swallowed outfielder Tom Goodwin's $3.5-million contract, and then they choked on it. After being released in spring training while remaining on the L.A. payroll, Goodwin was acquired by the Giants and promoted when a rash of injuries felled the outfield.

At Dodger Stadium, July 19-21, he really bit the hand that fed him. Replacing injured Barry Bonds in the 11th inning of the series opener, Goodwin hit a tie-breaking single in the 12th for a 3-2 victory, Dusty Baker's 800th as a manager.

That wasn't all. Starting for Bonds two days later, he did an imitation of his slugging teammate in the series finale, blasting a two-run homer of Giovanni Carrara in the eighth inning for a 6-4 victory before 54,344.

"The check is probably going to be a little late this week," Goodwin mused after telling Bonds, who was taking practice swings in the clubhouse, not to bother. "I told Barry not to put his pants on—I told him I'd take care of it."

Candlestick:
Home of the Giants, Beatles, Pope:

40 Turbulent Years in the Ballpark People Loved to Hate

A Matter of Time

National League president Chub Feeney, then the general manager of the Giants, made an inspection tour of Candlestick Park during its construction. When he headed toward the ballpark site, it was a bright and sunny day, ideal baseball weather.

While he was checking out the Giants' new digs, the wind began gusting around the steel and concrete, and Feeney curiously asked a construction worker: "Does it always blow like this around here?"

"Oh, no," the hard-hatter replied, "only between one and five in the afternoon." Feeney must have turned pale. He was well aware the Giants played mostly day games, and usually between those hours.

Years later, an enterprising reporter asked a weather expert when was the ideal time for conditions at Candlestick Point. The reply was an unpractical 4:00 a.m.

The Wind Made Me Do It

Candlestick Park's notorious wind first earned national disdain when the Giants hosted one of the two 1961 All-Star Games. Stu Miller, the club's diminutive and skilled reliever, was nudged slightly by a gust, a balk was called, and the incident lived in infamy among Candlestick lore.

"There was no wind that day until about the fifth inning," Miller recalled. "Then the flag started fluttering and was almost

Candlestick Park opened in 1960 and was the home of the Giants until the team moved into Pac Bell Park at the beginning of the 2000 season. (AP/ WWP)

torn off the flagpole by the time I got in. It was actually the windiest day I'd ever seen there. So, I came in an anchored myself, as usual.

"I got ready to throw to the hitter and went into my stretch position. Just then, an extra shot of wind came along, moving me some four to six inches. Nobody said anything, and I went ahead and delivered the pitch to Rocky Colavito.

"He swung and missed a slow curveball, and I could hear the American League bench hollering, 'Balk!' Stan Landes, the umpire, then motions the runner from second to third. I explained that the wind made me balk, but he said that rules are rules."

The fact that Miller was the winner of the game was obscured by the balk. He opened the newspapers the next day and was greeted by headlines like: "Miller Blown Off Mound." People remember that more than the fact he was 14-5 with a 2.66 ERA that season, earning NL Fireman of the Year distinction.

Paul Richards, AL manager during that fateful All-Star Game at The Stick, summed up what a lot of first-time visitors felt about the Giants' celebrated wind tunnel: "The wind, you have to feel it to believe it. Conditions were as near impossible as anything I've seen."

Just ask Stu Miller, who struck out nine batters in four and one-third innings—including Mickey Mantle, Roy Sievers and Elston Howard in succession—in the two All-Star Games that year, only to be linked forever with an unfortunate gust of wind.

A Festive Opener

The Giants opened $15-million Candlestick Park on April 12, 1960, when Sam Jones fired a three-hitter and Orlando Cepeda knocked in all the runs in a 3-1 victory over the St. Louis Cardinals before 42,269 and a host of dignitaries.

And it didn't take long for the notorious Candlestick wind to become a factor. Cepeda's wind-tortured, 410-foot drive eluded center fielder Bill White's grasp in the first inning and fell for a two-run triple, giving Jones all the support he required.

It was a busy day for White, who was traded for Jones the previous season. White, who was to become National League president, had two of the Cardinals' three hits and the first in the new stadium, which opened to rave reviews.

Vice President Richard Nixon, who once insisted "I am not a liar," was in attendance and obviously twisted the truth a tad by declaring: "San Francisco can say this is the finest ballpark in America."

An Ominous Sign

That Candlestick Park wouldn't be ideal for right-handed power hitters was evident immediately. During a workout the day prior to the historic opener, neither Willie Mays nor Orlando Cepeda could clear the fence.

In fact, among all the cuts taken by the Giants that day, only three balls left the yard—one each by left-handed hitters Dale Long, Matty Alou and Jim Marshall. Long knocked the first pitch of batting practice out, and then the wind wreaked havoc.

"Move the fences in!" Mays shouted following two rounds of BP. "This has got to be my defensive year. It looks like I'm in for a pay cut next year. There aren't going to be many home runs in this park."

Added Cepeda: "It's too far to left against the wind—I'll have to hit away." Of course, Cepeda had natural power to right-center from the start, but it was a bigger adjustment for Mays, who finished 1960 with 29 home runs.

When the first game was played the next day, their worst fears were realized. Mays hit a 397-foot drive to right center, but it was off the fence for a double. Cepeda smashed a 420-footer into White's glove at the fence.

"I thought it was going over," Cepeda said, shaking his head in disbelief. Added manager Bill Rigney: "Orlando's ball couldn't have been hit any harder." Such frustration was commonplace before The Stick was enclosed in 1972.

A Memory That Sticks

Giants catcher Jack Hiatt decided to have some fun when Bobby Bonds first joined the club, so he picked a typically windy day to take the young outfielder's uniform and glove and place them on the chain-link fence in right field.

"It was blowing so hard, they stuck," Bobby recalled. "I asked Jack how was I going to play right field, and he said, 'You're already out there.' It was so cold, none of us enjoyed playing on those tough nights."

The Beatles, the Stones, and the Pope

Besides baseball and football, Candlestick Park has been used for a wide range of events, the most notable being concerts staged by the Beatles and the Rolling Stones and a mass conducted by Pope John Paul II.

The Beatles created a buzz in 1966 with what would be their final concert, Aug. 29. While John, Paul, George and Ringo signed autographs in the clubhouse, adoring fans screamed in anticipation. "It's a bit chilly," John Lennon told the crowd.

Lennon, who once created controversy by suggesting the Beatles were more popular than Jesus, was proven wrong—in Candlestick Park, at least—on Sept. 18, 1987. That's when the Pontifical Mass attracted 70,000.

Security was tight for all three events, and a bulletproof "Popemobile" and altar were used for the 90-minute mass before His Holiness was whisked away—and not before Giants catcher Mike Sadek, an autograph hound, had a baseball signed, "J. P. II."

"It's the only one of its kind in the world," Sadek proudly boasted. "I have it in a safe. I sent Monsignor Lacey the ball, and Pope John signed it on their plane ride to San Francisco."

Tell It Goodbye

A crowd of 61,389, the largest regular-season baseball crowd in Candlestick Park, showed up for a funeral on Sept. 30, 1999. But it was more like an Irish wake as nostalgic fans celebrated the Giants' final game at the much-maligned 40-year-old stadium. The Dodgers posted a 9-4 victory, but it really didn't matter.

This was about saying goodbye to an old friend, and the distinguished guest list included Hall of Famers Willie Mays, Juan Marichal, Willie McCovey and Orlando Cepeda. "This is a World Series without a World Series," Giants manager Dusty Baker said.

Marvin Benard hit the Giants' final home run at The Stick, and Jeff Kent's bases-loaded walk gave him 100 RBI. Raul Mondesi homered and drove in four runs for the Dodgers. Eric Karros said: "The weather is the nicest I've seen at Candlestick. If it was like this all the time, nobody would want to leave."

The three-game series attracted 143,518 paying customers, bringing the season total to 2,078,365, at the time the second highest total in S.F. history. The Giants' final record at The Stick was 1,775-1,398.

The Final Chapter

When the Giants finally concluded their controversial 40-year run at Candlestick Point with a 3-2 loss to the Dodgers, Hall of Famers Willie Mays, Willie McCovey and Juan Marichal held the majority of the ballpark's records.

McCovey was No. 1 at The Stick in games (1,085), at-bats (3,369), hits (925), home runs (236) and RBI (698). Mays was tops in runs (598) and doubles (161), and second in most other categories. The figures included their games with other teams.

Marichal dominated the pitching charts, ranking first in innings (1,7082/3), wins (122) and strikeouts (1,144). The father-son duo of Bobby and Barry Bonds ranked one-two in stolen bases with 141 and 114, respectively.

Among opponents, Pete Rose had the most games (172), at-bats (681), runs (85) and hits (201). Dale Murphy and Willie Stargell tied for the home run lead with 25, Ron Cey had a high of 76 RBI, and Joe Morgan had the most stolen bases with 48.

The winningest opposing pitcher was Phil Niekro (15), followed by Tom Seaver (13), Burt Hooton (12), Bob Gibson (12), Don Sutton (11), and Steve Carlton (11). All are Hall of Famers except Hooton. Hideo Nomo's 1.22 ERA shaded Kevin Brown's 1.31.

Tell Us What You Really Think

Following is a variety of criticism elicited by the capricious climate of Candlestick Park:

"I got prepared for Candlestick by putting down all the windows in my car, taking off my jacket and driving around San Francisco."
—*Dusty Baker*

"We used to feel sorry for the fans, not for ourselves. We saw them sitting in the stands, freezing at night games, and wondered how they did it. At least we were moving around on the field."
—*Willie McCovey*

"It would be like putting lipstick on a pig."
—*Fran Healy on the prospect of doming Candlestick Park*

"I think a lot of people from an atomic waste plant explosion filtered into San Francisco. I think they put all the mutant people there. They hit you with rocks, bottles and cans the whole game. You feel like you're at a carnival and people are throwing balls at you."
—*Rob Dibble*

"We're lucky. We can leave here after a short series, but the Giants have to stay here all the time."
—*Lew Burdette*

"Chewing tobacco and sand isn't a tasty combination."
—*Hoyt Wilhelm*

"The trouble with this ballpark is that they built it alongside the bay. They should have built it under the bay."
—*Roger Maris*

"Candlestick Park is the grossest error in the history of major-league baseball...the ballpark slants toward the bay—in fact, it slides toward the bay and before long will be under water, which is the best place for it."
—*Jim Brosnan in* **Pennant Race**

"It's like trying to hit a cotton ball wearing an overcoat—no one from Candlestick will ever win a batting championship."
—*Bill Madlock*

"The only difference between Candlestick and San Quentin is that at Candlestick they let you go home at night."
—*Jim Wohlford*

"Dynamite."
—*Jack Clark, when asked what would improve Candlestick*

"Playing at Candlestick is like playing on the deck of the carrier *Enterprise* in the South China Sea."
—*Giants executive Pat Gallagher*

"When the ball is hit to me in left field, I try to catch the middle of the three balls that are coming at me."
—*Harvey Kuenn*

"Sitting in the dugout is like sitting in the bottom of a toilet. All that tissue blows in, and no one flushes it."
—*Whitey Herzog*

"Until I played at Candlestick, I never realized how great Willie Mays must have been. My God, what would he have done in a real ballpark?"
—*Ozzie Smith*

"The wind blows, the fog rolls in. If that's not exciting enough, they ought to just plant land mines arbitrarily in the outfield."
—Joe Magrane

"If I had to play here, I'd think seriously about quitting the game."
—*Rocky Colavito at the 1961 All-Star Game*

"When Pittsburgh came in, Clemente would play one game and sit two."
—*Willie Mays*

"Don't blame the architect. After all, it's his first ballpark."
—*Columnist Herb Caen on developer Charles Harney*

"You had to learn to hit and field with your eyes watering. You always checked the schedule and prayed for day games."
—*Davey Johnson*

"Distressingly, this may have been the best chance we had of getting rid of this ballpark."
—*Announcer Hank Greenwald shortly after the 1989 earthquake*

"Maybe the solution is to play only one game a year here and invite a million to attend."

—Bobby Murcer on solving attendance problems
"How the Giants manage to play 77 games a year in this wind is beyond me. Why, you've got to be a circus performer just to catch a pop fly."
—Yankees coach Frankie Crosetti at the 1961 All-Star Game

"Good riddance. I don't even want to look at a postcard of this stadium."
—Rick Monday during the final series in 1999

"It would be kind of like dropping an aspirin tablet in a toilet, then flushing and trying to grab it with a pair of tweezers."
—Bob Brenly on catching pop flies at Candlestick Park

The Bad and the Ugly

Taunts and Tussles

The First Big Brawl

It was May, 25, 1958, when the Giants visited Pittsburgh and swept a doubleheader from the Pirates, 5-2 and 6-1, behind the pitching of Ruben Gomez and Ramon Monzant. Tension was high because the previous season, Gomez struck Pirates pitcher Vern Law on the left ear with a pitch, rupturing his eardrum and knocking him out for the season.

So, it was predictable what would happen after Gomez buzzed Frank Thomas with a pitch in the fourth inning of the opener. Umpire Frank Dascoli issued a warning to the Giants' pitcher, but two batters later, Gomez plunked Bill Mazeroski and all hell broke loose before 35,797, the second largest crowd in Forbes Field history.

"I had an 0-2 count on him," Gomez recalled, "and in that situation, I used to brush the guy back and then came back with a curve. But I hung the curve, and he fouled it deep to left. I decided to brush him back, and I came too close."

Mazeroski raised his hand, deflecting the pitch from his head, and began yelling at Gomez, who batted in the fifth. Law's first pitch sent him sprawling, and Dascoli issued another warning. Murtaugh charged Gomez, who swung at the manager with his bat.

"Thank God, he ducked," Gomez said. "I took the hat right off his head with the swing. I would have cracked his head open. I'd have been in jail until now [1998]. He got up and started screaming, 'This guy's crazy.' Then someone else came after me."

Murtaugh was then grabbed by third base coach Herman Franks and the benches emptied. That's when Willie Mays alertly made what might have been the play of the year.

Rookie Orlando Cepeda, rushing to the aide of his friend and mentor Gomez, grabbed a bat and headed for the melee. Mays tackled him to avert further trouble, and Gomez was allowed to continue while Murtaugh was ejected, adding to the Pirates' chagrin.

"In the corner of my eye, I saw Cepeda charge out of the dugout with a bat," Mays said. "I'm saying to myself, 'No, no, that can't happen,' so I tackled him. But he's so strong, I couldn't keep him down.

"I had to pin him down on the ground, and then I saw a body come over the top of me. It was Hank Sauer. Then we pinned him down together."

Mays to the Mound?

Veteran right-hander Bob Purkey had a penchant for attempting to discourage Willie Mays by throwing brushback pitches to the Giants' superstar. Following such an incident, manager Bill Rigney decided to do something about it when he attended the 1959 All-Star Game in Pittsburgh the next week.

"I ran into [commissioner] Ford Frick and [NL president] Warren Giles, and I've had about three Bloody Marys," Rig recalled. "So, I asked them if I could speak with them for a moment, and they asked what was on my mind.

"I just want to get on record. The next time my team comes into Cincinnati, Bob Purkey is going to pitch against us. And what's going to happen is the first time that Mays gets up, Purkey is going to knock him down.

"And then Mays is going to make an out, or maybe go oh for four. I want to go on record that when Purkey goes up to hit, I'm going to take Willie out of center field, bring him to the mound and he's going to knock Purkey's hat off!"

Well, the Giants soon visited Cincinnati, and Don Newcombe was pitching against Ramon Monzant. Mays was buzzed by Big Newk, so when the Reds' pitcher came to bat, Rigney yelled: "You better keep that helmet down low under your ears!"

Rising to the challenge, the unintimidated Newcombe walked over to the Giants' dugout and sternly told Rigney: "If he [Monzant] comes close to me, I'm coming over here to get you!"

Monzant didn't come close, averting a brawl and giving the Reds a moral victory. But Cincinnati didn't make Mays hit the dirt the rest of the season, so Rigney finally had made his point.

Sauer Turns Sour

Hank Sauer was the first man to homer in the L.A. Coliseum when the Dodgers played their first game there in 1958. "Honker" was a 41-year-old spare outfielder with the 1959 Giants when he volunteered to become a coach late that season to save a roster spot for young Felipe Alou, who balked at returning to the minors.

Late in September, after a sweep by the Dodgers knocked the Giants one game out of first place, the club shifted to Wrigley Field, and Sauer, the 1952 MVP with the Cubs, knew there was some chicanery going on in the huge center field scoreboard.

"The Cubs were stealing our signs," Sauer said. "Nobody ever hit Sam Jones's curveball the way they were hitting him that day [George Altman hit a game-winning homer in the ninth as dusk descended].

"I could see they were relaying our signs from the scoreboard down to the field, so I told Bill Rigney, 'Let me get dressed, and I'll go up there and throw that telescope right out that window.'

"Well, I went up there and started pounding on the door. They wouldn't let me in, so I yelled, 'If I get up there, you're going to find out how quick I can throw all three of you through those portholes!' We're trying to win a pennant and they had nowhere to go, but they knocked us out of a pennant by doing it."

A Boxing Doubleheader

In his first 11 years as a major-leaguer, Willie Mays never got into a scrape on the field. That all changed, May 27, 1962, when the Mets visited Candlestick Park and 39,511 were in attendance, many to see New York manager Casey Stengel.

It was a baseball doubleheader swept by the Giants 7-1, 6-5, with a boxing twin-bill thrown in. During the seventh inning of the opener there were two ugly confrontations involving Orlando Cepeda with Roger Craig and Mays with Elio Chacon.

The Cepeda-Craig clash truly was a battle of heavyweights. Craig, who would become Giants' manager 23 years later, weighed in at six-foot-four and 200 pounds. The aptly-named Baby Bull also was 200 pounds.

Craig twice decked Mays in the first inning, setting the tone. In the seventh, he struck Cepeda's left shoulder with a pitch. Cepeda, bat in hand, started toward the mound before heading for first base, from where he and Craig began glaring at each other.

Suddenly, Cepeda bolted for the mound and was tackled by manager Alvin Dark, a former football player at LSU. Dark and coach Wes Westrum pinned Cepeda down and Mays, on second, also headed toward the mound to intercept the raging Bull.

Craig claimed Cepeda instigated the bench-clearing brawl by yelling from first base: "I get you for this!" The Mets' pitcher then reportedly shot back: "Why didn't you do it when you had a bat in your hand?"

Round Two to Mays

Soon after order was restored from the Cepeda-Craig flareup in the seventh inning, Mays returned to second base, where Craig attempted to pick him off. Following the second throw, Mays slid back safely and second baseman Elio Chacon began hitting him on the head.

Enraged for one of the few times in his career, the 190-pound Mays jumped to his feet, picked up the lightweight Chacon by his hips and slammed him to the ground, where he landed several punches before being pulled away.

Chacon claimed Mays spiked him scrambling back to second, and there definitely was some history between them. In 1961, Chacon was with the Cincinnati Reds, when he was spiked above the right knee by Mays at Candlestick and required 10 stitches.

"If I'd known he was carrying a grudge, I'd have done things differently," Mays said. "I don't know why he started hitting me. All I was trying to do was protect myself. I wish I'd known he was going to do it. I'd have been prepared—not to hit him, but to keep him from hitting me."

While Mays and Chacon fought, Cepeda and Craig again went at it, each missing on punches as the Bull pursued the retreating pitcher. Only Chacon was ejected, and he eventually was fined $100.

Craig continued, but Felipe Alou followed with a two-run single, placing the game out of reach. Alou was five for eight in the sweep with three runs, three steals and six RBI.

Just Kidding, Fellas

Catchers Dick Dietz and Jack Hiatt once had reporters convinced they had a bloody clubhouse fight, but it merely was one of those frequent pranks that kept the players loose and drove manager Clyde King daffy.

"We faked a fight," Dietz explained. "It was a Giants-Dodgers game and there was always a lot of press around. Jack and I lockered close to each other, and we made it up that I was going to go over and tell him he'd played a lousy game.

"And he'd pretend to get mad. I had gone to get a handful of ketchup, and he gave the ol' fake POW! Then I hit myself with the ketchup, and we looked up and saw the reporters writing up a storm. They all believed it, and then we started laughing."

Slugfest at the Springs

One of the wildest spring training brawls broke out in Palm Springs, where the California Angels hosted the Giants in 1971. Tito Fuentes was struck by a Clyde Wright pitch and words were exchanged as the Giants' infielder headed toward first base. Benches cleared and several fights erupted.

Rookie pitcher Jim Barr recalled the melee, but from a far different perspective—from his hotel room.

"A bunch of us had pitched in a B game that morning, so we were back at the team hotel," Barr said. "I was taking a shower, and one of the guys yells, 'Quick, come here!' I got out and went into the other room and looked at the TV.

"There was a policeman standing on the field, and we wondered what was going on. Turns out there was a Pier 6 brawl with a lot of guys involved. Dave Kingman had [coach] John Roseboro in a headlock, but nobody was seriously hurt."

Giants catcher Mike Sadek was in the bullpen that day, and he suggested Barr was being conservative.

"There were two rounds," Sadek recalled, "and I saw Bobby Bonds lifting one of the Angels and pin him to the fence. And Kingman was hitting Roseboro all over. Roseboro might have been a tough guy, but not against Kingman, who was the strongest guy I ever saw."

Not So Fast, Mac

During a brawl between the Giants and the Chicago Cubs in 1972, Willie McCovey approached rival first baseman Joe Pepitone, who was holding his bat a safe distance from the combat zone.

Pepitone felt a tap on the shoulder, turned to face the menacing McCovey and blurted: "Hey, Willie Mac, I'm on your side. I like the guys on your team more than the guys on mine."

The Count vs. Bristol

When John Montefusco taunted opponents with his boasts, he was seldom taken seriously by those aware of his playful nature. But The Count was all business when he marched into manager Dave Bristol's office, June 18, 1980, miffed over being lifted in the ninth inning of an 8-5 victory over the New York Mets at Candlestick Park.

The door to Bristol's office was closed for 10 minutes as their angry voices escalated. When players rushed to separate the combatants, Montefusco had his manager in a headlock, but it was the pitcher who sported a black eye.

"I didn't want to be hitting a 40-year-old man," said Montefusco, 30. "I kept backing off, but after he suckered me, I got him in a headlock and was about to knock the crap out of him when we were separated.

"Bristol provoked it. He didn't like what I was saying, and he told me to get out of his office. I was backing up, and he kept pushing and pushing. I told him, 'You'd better stop it or I'll deck you.' He kept pushing me until he sucker-punched me."

Bristol's version: "I did what I had to do. I don't want anyone screaming at me, telling me this and that. I told him to keep quiet, and he just kept going on and on. It had to be done sooner or later. You can't get into a situation where a player is dictating to a manager."

Will Wasn't Alone

Prior to Will Clark's arrival as Jeffrey Leonard's constant whipping boy, the feisty Giants outfielder scuffled with teammates Dan Gladden and Jim Gott. During batting practice in Cincinnati, April 19, 1985, Gladden took exception to some ribbing and the pair fought behind the cage at home plate.

"That was stupid—I was yelling at Dan, and he had to do something," recalled Leonard, who resigned as team captain following the incident. "If I let that knucklehead get me that upset, I don't need to be captain."

The flareup was provoked, according to Mike Krukow, "because Danny was one of those guys who would milk batting practice, fouling off balls and taking extra cuts, and that ticked off Hac. He kept riding him in front of everybody and backed Danny into a corner."

That day, Gladden got Leonard's goat by being late for batting practice. They exchanged unpleasantries, and when Leonard left the batting cage he told his teammate he didn't want to talk with him the rest of the season, emphatically poking Gladden's chest in the process.

Suddenly, Gladden jumped the bigger Leonard and knocked him down. When order was restored, Gladden refused to discuss the altercation, but an embarrassed Leonard fessed up following the Reds' 4-2 victory.

"That will be the last time anybody on this team, or any team, jumps in my face," he vowed. "I wasn't thinking of doing anything physical, so I didn't try to hit him. But I'll take the blame, I think I was more in the wrong."

Getting to Gott

Jim Gott was a mild-mannered and affable pitcher in his days with the Giants, but appearances were deceiving. Gott was a martial arts expert and obviously the wrong man to mess with when Jeff Leonard took exception to the pitcher wearing sunglasses in the dugout during a night game at Shea Stadium in May of 1986.

"That's book!" shouted Leonard, meaning Gott would have to pay a fine in the club's kangaroo court. The pitcher didn't appreciate the ragging or the punishment, so he and Leonard engaged in a shoving match and had to be separated by teammates, which may have been Leonard's good fortune.

"Gott would have killed him," Mike Krukow recalled. "He was about six foot four and 245 pounds with about six percent body fat—an animal. You did not mess with him. He got Jeff in a compromising position and scared the hell out of him."

The Giants weren't angered by the incident, but didn't appreciate a cameraman airing their dirty linen. Leonard explained: "We were getting our butts kicked, and I didn't like him trying to be cool with those shades." Added Gott: "Hac was always testing you, and he got to me in New York."

Not for long.

A Busch Brawl

One of the lengthiest brawls in the Giants' recent history occurred July 22, 1986, during a 10-7 St. Louis Cardinals victory at Busch Stadium. What triggered it was Vince Coleman stealing second and third base in the fifth inning with the home club holding a 10-2 lead.

Coleman was tagged out at the plate by pitcher Juan Berenguer, who spiked the ball and yelled at the Cardinals' speedster, who was shooting for a stolen base record. When Coleman batted in the seventh, Frank Williams's pitch came close to him, and plate umpire Bob Davidson issued a warning.

The next pitch struck Coleman, automatically ejecting Williams and manager Roger Craig. Giants third baseman Chris Brown had to be restrained and both benches cleared. Giants pitcher Mike Krukow charged Coleman, who tackled him.

Meanwhile, Craig and Cardinals manager Whitey Herzog were yelling and pushing each other, and a scrum ensued near the backstop screen. Tom Herr sustained an eight-stitch gash near his left ear, and Herzog scuffled with Joel Youngblood and Randy Kutcher.

"We don't stop running when we're eight runs down in the fifth inning," said Herzog, who was somewhat justified in giving Coleman the green light because the Giants rallied with three runs in the eighth and threatened in the ninth. "I told him [Craig] we're going to run in the fifth inning. I'll never stop running now against that sucker."

Déjà vu in St. Lou

The Giants had a heated NLCS at Busch in 1987, and tempers flared once again when they visited the Cardinals' ballpark on July 24, 1988. This time, St. Louis second baseman Jose Oquendo took exception to a hard slide by Will Clark that broke up a double play in the eighth.

Clark, whose three-run homer in the fifth powered a 5-0 victory, was playing aggressive baseball, according to the Giants. Herzog saw it as an illegal slide attempting to injure Oquendo, who kneed Clark in retaliation and took a swipe at the runner's helmet.

It became a full-scale brawl when shortstop Ozzie Smith rushed behind Clark, taking a swing at the back of his head. Candy Maldonado, who was on first, bolted to second along with coach Dusty Baker and jumped on the pile.

"The fastest I've ever seen Candy go from first to second," Craig quipped.

Smith and Bob Brenly were jawing heatedly before order was restored. Not for long. Reliever Scott Terry's second pitch sailed over Mike Aldrete's head, and the benches cleared again.

Cardinals catcher Tom Pagnozzi, citing Clark as the instigator, said: "If Clark continues to slide like that, somebody will take care of him...Somebody might drop down [with a throw] and smoke his noggin."

Clark's version: "He [Oquendo] kneed me and slapped the back of my head, and it wasn't playful. When the fists started flying, I got one good uppercut in, and then I wound up at the bottom of the pile."

Brenly, who rushed from the bullpen, enjoyed squaring off with Smith, drawing some blood from the the Wizard and explaining with satisfaction: "I don't know if somebody stepped on him or what—maybe his lip got caught rolling over on my hand."

Hac-Man vs. The Thrill

The Giants usually saved their aggression for other teams, namely the archrival Dodgers, but there have been hostilities within their clubhouse, including the brittle Barry Bonds-Jeff Kent relationship and the fight between manager Dave Bristol and John Montefusco. But they paled in comparison to the ongoing feud between Jeffrey Leonard and Will Clark.

It began as soon as Clark arrived on the scene in 1986, not far removed from the Mississippi State campus. Leonard, a clubhouse leader, sensed Clark's confidence and made sure to test the rookie with taunts and clubhouse pranks. They weren't well received, and Clark was relieved when Hac-Man was traded in 1988.

"He was a tumor," Clark declared. "We got rid of him, and now look where we are. He was a jealous ballplayer. He couldn't understand why a player was called up and got all the attention, so he made my life miserable. The stuff he did [to me] didn't have anything to do with baseball.

"Hac was a real pain in the rear. He just loved playing the role of the intimidator. He was very rough on me, going beyond the call of duty, and I resented it. I remember going on the disabled list, and my first day back in the clubhouse, all my bats were in the trash can.

"It got to me, but I couldn't let him know it. That's what he wanted. Then I did the same thing with his bats when he went on the DL, and he just laughed about it."

Leonard, no shrinking violet, responded and gave a detailed account of a clubhouse scuffle with Clark in Philadelphia, and also recalled how Clark berated African-American teammate Chris Brown and was compelled to apologize in front of the entire team.

"Will is a talented hitter, but he's prejudiced," Leonard said. "My nephew approached him in Philly and asked for an autograph. Will told him to get his [butt] out of there. The next day, they had to pull me off him in the clubhouse.

"Will's racial remarks went down all the time. He actually called Chris a [bleep] to his face. Those are personality flaws in Will's character. I hope by now that he's cleared them up. I rode him hard because I wanted to see what he was made of."

Catcher Bob Brenly added: "Will had an attitude about certain things, and Hac didn't let him slide by. He tested Will like crazy, finding his vulnerability and riding him unmercifully."

A Crossbay Rivalry

The Giants-A's rivalry heated up during the late 1980s, when each club had young stars like Will Clark, Matt Williams, Kevin Mitchell, Mark McGwire and Jose Canseco. The neighborhood rivalry heated up during the 1989 World Series, an Oakland sweep. By then, Clark and Canseco were the stars of their respected teams, and Canseco couldn't resist taunting his crossbay counterpart.

"Will Clark, you big dummy," Canseco said. "I'm making a million more than you are. You overrated, slow, three-toed sloth with no arms. You hear me, boy?"

The Gasmouth Gang

There was no love lost when the Giants engaged the Cardinals in the 1987 NLCS, and Jeffrey Leonard stirred the St. Louis fans with home runs in each of the first four games. When the Giants took a 3-2 lead in the best-of-seven series, the action returned to Busch Stadium, where Leonard and his teammates heard the wrath of the Cardinals and their red-clad followers.

Whereas Leonard enraged them with his flap-down home run trot, teammate Chili Davis really hit a sensitive nerve when he called St. Louis "a cowtown." Sure enough, the fired-up fans brought clanging cowbells to Busch, frequently serenading the Giants while back-to-back shutouts gave the Cardinals the pennant.

"He's so dumb, he thinks milk comes from ants," Cardinals coach Red Schoendienst said of Davis. But most of the anger was reserved for Leonard, the target of jeers and some biting comments from infielder Tommy Herr, who summed up: "He tried to intimidate us, show us up the whole series. He can take the MVP; we'll take the World Series."

Shortstop Ozzie Smith, who had a history of run-ins with the Giants, also couldn't resist a dig or two, declaring: "What the Giants have done all series is classless. They came in here like they were the greatest thing since cornflakes. It looks like they came to talk; we came to play."

Mitchell's Mayhem

It didn't take long for Kevin Mitchell to establish his slugging prowess in 1991. He homered Opening Day against the host San Diego Padres, and he did likewise in the second inning of Game 2, April 10, against left-hander Bruce Hurst.

On his next at-bat, Mitchell became agitated over a high inside pitch and started toward the mound. He was intercepted by manager Roger Craig and order temporarily was restored. When the next pitch struck his foot, Mitchell went ballistic.

The five-foot-11, 210-pound Mitchell lowered his shoulder and charged the mound like a furious bull. He knocked over the six-foot-three, 219-pound Hurst and was prevented from doing more damage because Padres first baseman Fred McGriff alertly tackled him.

"I owe Fred a dinner—he probably saved my life," Hurst said following the Padres' 5-3 victory. Added McGriff: "Kevin was gonna kill him. I know Mitch from the minors, and I've never seen him so angry. I just instinctively got in his way."

Padres manager Greg Riddoch called Mitchell a raging bull, and Will Clark didn't argue, observing: "I've seen Mitch get mad before, but nothing like this. I think you could have put a brick wall out there and he would have run right through it."

A Rocky Relationship

Although the Dodgers are the Giants' archrivals, there have been many more heated disputes with the Colorado Rockies since the expansion team was born in 1993. Most of them occurred when Dusty Baker and Don Baylor, purportedly good friends, were managing against each other.

It didn't take long for the ill will to fester. In the ninth inning of an 8-2 Giants victory at Mile High Stadium, May 12, 1993, Mike Jackson struck Jerald Clark with a pitch, touching off a brawl in which Barry Bonds dashed to the aid of his father, Bobby, who was going at it with fellow coach Ron Hassey.

Both Bondses, Hassey and Jackson were ejected. The next spring in Tucson, Robby Thompson was hit on the batting helmet by a Mike Harkey pitch and missed several games. Tempers escalated because Thompson was recovering from a shattered cheekbone (the result of a Trevor Hoffman pitch) the previous September.

It kept getting uglier in the summer of '94. On June 25, Salomon Torres hit Andres Galarraga and Charlie Hayes on consecutive pitches. Hayes, whose jaw was fractured by the pitch, had to be restrained by Baylor during a wild melee. On July 28, Dave Burba hit Dante Bichette and Galarraga on consecutive pitches, fracturing the latter's right hand.

When the two clubs played again three days later, Rockies pitcher Jim Czajkowski struck Royce Clayton and Kirt Manwaring on successive at-bats, and Baker had to restrain Clayton from charging the mound. On April 13, 1995, Galarraga was hit on the right forearm by Jose Bautista in spring training, the last straw for Baylor.

"We've seen too much of that," he steamed following the post-strike exhibition opener. "We're going to make a statement [retaliation]. Our pitchers will start going inside, and it's going to be in the middle of the [Giants'] lineup. We have to take a different approach with them."

Baker, not appreciating the threat, responded: "Why would anyone want to hit Galarraga? He has an unorthodox stance, he crowds the plate and he dives into pitches. I think he needs to know how to get out of the way. Are we the only team which hits him?"

The bad blood ebbed for a while, and it was curious that Hayes and Galarraga would one day become members of the Giants. Galarraga, in fact, played a key role down the stretch for the 2001 Giants and was invited to spring training with them in 2003.

A Front Office Feud

The Giants and crossbay A's have never had a significant disagreement on the field, but there has been a not-so-friendly feud among the front offices of both Bay Area teams, partly because of frustration born of two teams competing for fans in the same region.

Until they moved into Pacific Bell Park, where sellouts are commonplace, the Giants' attendance was affected by the presence of the A's. Each team has wished the other would disappear, and it almost happened on more than one occasion.

Marketing departments have become involved, and the A's in 2000 had the following billboard advertisement on the Oakland approach to the Bay Bridge: "While They're Building a Stadium, We're Building a Team." That low blow capitalized on the fact that the Giants had a new ballpark, but that the A's had the championships—four World Series to none—since each moved to California.

At the annual 2000 Fox preseason luncheon, A's manager Art Howe listened to Giants counterpart Dusty Baker convey his wish for a ticker-tape parade. When it was his turn to speak, Howe told Baker: "We'll invite you."

That was in a humorous vein, but the jabbing by A's executives was more mean-spirited. There was a standing joke about the Giants building a new ballpark, but not requiring a trophy room.

When Sandy Alderson was president and general manager of the A's, he once quipped at a press gathering, "There's nothing more boring than golf on radio ... except the Giants on television."

That was said in jest, but Alderson wasn't kidding when he chastised the Giants for giving Barry Bonds a $22.9 million contract extension prior to the 1997 season.

"That's just a bribe to keep his mouth shut," Alderson said. "These kind of things affect us all...a very disturbing trend...we've tried to run our team the way we think is appropriate. This just makes it easier to ignore the way they run their team."

"The A's ought to worry about the A's—they're not going that good," Giants GM Brian Sabean fired back. And when Pacific Bell Park was opened in 2000, the Giants cancelled the annual Bay Bridge Series exhibitions with the A's, instead inviting the Brewers and Yankees for the festivities.

Hayes vs. Stottlemyre

The Diamondbacks pounded the Giants 10-4 in the opener of a weekend series at Bank One Ballpark, April 16, 1999, and most of the attention was on Arizona pitcher Todd Stottlemyre and S.F. third baseman Charlie Hayes, who scuffled near the mound over an apparent lack of communication.

Hayes hit into a forceout in the sixth and insisted he was cussing at himself when Stottlemyre thought the expletives were directed at him. After Hayes reached second base on Brent Mayne's single, Stottlemyre was yelling, and Arizona second baseman Jay Bell said the pitcher was upset over allowing a hit. Hayes interpreted it differently.

Suddenly, Hayes and Stottlemyre were heading for each other. Giants coach Sonny Jackson tackled Stottlemyre, and Arizona third baseman Matt Williams had Hayes pinned. Benches cleared, both combatants were ejected, and Barry Bonds restrained Hayes, who was escorted off the field.

"I just don't like him," Hayes said in a masterful piece of understatement. "Nobody likes him because he's an ass. He should just pitch and keep his mouth shut. If he has a problem with me, we can get it settled. I tried to hurt him. He talks too much. He talks like he's Bob Gibson. I'm the only guy who can't hit him."

Hayes was referring to his lack of success against the pitcher and the fact he missed with a punch when the fight started, to which Stottlemyre responded: "He missed me all night, at the plate and on the mound. He had something to say to me at first base, and I had something to say back to him at second."

When order was restored, Arizona ace Randy Johnson inadvertently provided some comic relief. The Big Unit straightened

his uniform, picked up a cap and placed it on his head—before
realizing in shock while adjusting it that it belonged to the Giants.

Rockies Horror Show

The long-standing feud between the Giants and Rockies flared
again in 2000. Buddy Bell replaced Don Baylor in the Colorado
dugout, and nothing really changed. The Giants were angered
May 12 at Coors Field when Tom Goodwin stole second base
with a 14-7 lead in the seventh of a game eventually won by the
home club 15-7.

Goodwin's dash was regarded as unsportsmanlike, according
to the so-called "unwritten rules" of baseball, so when a similar
situation arose at Coors Field in the opener of a four-game series,
June 26, it got ugly. That night, Goodwin stole his league-leading 35th base with a seven-run lead in the seventh inning of a 15-
6 Rockies romp.

The next night, Shawn Estes, coasting to a 12-7 victory, sent
a "message pitch" to Goodwin in the eighth inning. It sailed behind Goodwin's head, and Bell rushed out of the dugout to protest to plate umpire Jerry Layne. After the short-tempered Bell
was ejected, he directed his venom toward the Giants' dugout
and Baker.

"It ain't over!" an irate Bell screamed at Baker and continued
his tirade following the game. "You don't throw at somebody's
head. As mad as I am right now, I wouldn't throw at one of the
Giants' heads."

"They have a coach [Robby Thompson] who almost got killed
[by a Trevor Hoffman fastball in 1993]. You'd think that would
have taught them a lesson, and it didn't. Headhunters are not
good for this game."

Baker was subdued in the Giants' clubhouse, but was irri-
tated by Bell's threat, saying: "When a guy says, 'It's not over,'
how am I supposed to take it? You don't get personal like that.
I've never been yelled at like that, not even by my father. I don't

want to see anyone suspended, but you can't let anyone punk you out, either."

Given the hitter-friendly conditions at Coors Field, most observers felt the Giants overreacted to Goodwin's theft. That was vividly demonstrated one night later, when the Giants took an 8-1 lead in the top of the third and were ahead 11-5 in the fifth before the Rockies rallied for a 17-13 victory.

Irritating Indian Dance

Mild-mannered Russ Davis usually didn't show much emotion, but a so-called "Indian dance" by Chicago Cubs pitcher Julian Tavarez ignited a curious exchange between the pair in an exhibition game at Mesa, March 26, 2001.

With two on and two outs in the third inning, Tavarez struck out Davis on a 2-2 pitch and expressed his glee with some gyrations. Davis took exception and tempers suddenly flared when the pair tangled down the first base line.

"I looked up and he was doing his dance," Davis said. "I said, 'What's that?'—and then he threw his stuff [cap and glove] down, and I had to do something. I didn't like him doing his Indian dance out there."

They clashed as Tavarez was heading toward the Cubs' dugout. The dugouts emptied and there was a pileup of players before order was restored. Both combatants were ejected, and the Cubs rolled to a 6-3 victory, after which the fiery pitcher was still steaming.

"Don't swear at me, don't open your mouth—I don't hear what you say, I don't read lips," Tavarez recalled what he said after Davis became upset, adding that he told him, "Oh, it's all right for you to hit a homer and admire it."

Blame It on Rios

Barry Bonds and Jeff Kent weren't the only Giants to scuffle in the team's dugout in San Diego. During a game with the Pa-

Jason Schmidt went on to become an important cog in the Giants'
starting rotation in 2002 after he was acquired in a trade for
Armando Rios in 2001. (Photo courtesy of the San Francisco Giants)

dres, June 21, 2001, tensions simmering between Rich Aurilia and Armando Rios surfaced in the sixth inning.

Aurilia, bothered by a sore toe, failed to tag and advance from second on a long drive by Jeff Kent. When he didn't score on Rios's single to right, Rios was upset. After Aurilia scored on a sacrifice fly, Rios and Calvin Murray were commenting on Aurilia's lack of speed.

Rios and Murray both had words with Aurilia, and a fight was avoided when Bonds and manager Dusty Baker restrained Rios, who played down the incident and called it "something stupid, no big deal."

Aurilia concurred, adding: "It's over with ... you're around guys all season, and people are gonna have their little run-ins. It's nothing serious. You can't dwell on it. Nobody's going to remember it in three weeks."

Rios was traded for Jason Schmidt the following month, and Baker called the in-house altercation "a misunderstanding," blaming the TV cameraman for taping it. "I wanted to kick his butt," Baker said. "But he was just doing his job, going for an Emmy—like catching a tornado."

A Family Feud

It wasn't unusual that an argument broke out when the Giants and the Diamondbacks were on the brink of a fight at Candlestick Park, July 22, 2001. What was odd was that Arizona third baseman Matt Williams nearly came to blows with his mentor, manager Dusty Baker.

Williams apparently angered the Giants by swinging on a 3-0 Kirk Rueter pitch with a 5-0 lead in the fifth inning and doubling against his former team. One inning later, a Chad Zerbe pitch sailed behind Williams's head.

The quick-tempered Williams took a few steps toward the mound and in three quick motions pointed to the scoreboard (Arizona was ahead 10-3), to Zerbe and the Giants' dugout. Players poured out of the dugouts and there was the usual milling and jawing.

Suddenly, a reddening Williams and Baker were having a heated argument near third base, and the manager had to be restrained by coach Gene Clines from going after his protege. Williams, once the darling of Giants fans, heard boos.

"What would you do if a guy was pointing a finger in your face?" Baker said after the 12-4 Arizona romp. "He was talking some [trash] and pointing his finger—that's a sign of aggression to me. I love Matty, and always will, but I don't like gestures toward me. I don't have a bad temper, but it's a short temper."

Williams, who went six for 12 in the series, didn't anticipate any problems in the return engagement with the Giants the following week. In fact, the contrite Williams phoned Baker prior to the next series and apologized.

"I haven't slept in four days," Williams said. "I told him what I felt about him, and that at the time I didn't think it was inappropriate to swing on 3-0. It bothers me that they were upset about it and that Dusty called me names, but we cleared the air."

Bonds vs. Kent

In the most overblown "fight" of the 2002, longtime adversaries Barry Bonds and Jeff Kent were involved in a shoving match in the Giants' Qualcomm Stadium dugout, June 25. Because of their stature and the fact that the flareup was captured on camera made for big news.

One Bay Area columnist foolishly insisted that Kent be traded on the spot, which management deftly dismissed. The incident occurred in the third inning when Bonds stepped in after Kent chided teammate David Bell for his judgment on a fielding play.

While they argued, Bonds told them to calm down. Then Bonds and Kent got into it with some shoves, and manager Dusty Baker rushed to intervene. Kent reportedly yelled: "I want off this team!" which set off the manager. Kent added: "It's his team anyway—of course, you'll take his side."

That the feud had no lasting effect was immediately evident. Bonds hit a three-run homer that inning, and Kent greeted him with a high-five before also homering in the sixth.

"It's no big deal," Kent insisted. "Just add it to the half a dozen times we've done it before. So much has been made about the relationship we have. I think we have a good working relationship."

Kent said after the wild-card clincher that the San Diego scuffle was beneficial, calling it "the turning point" of the season because it brought the team together.

"It showed the guys on the team, the front office and the fans how much we really cared," he explained. "We weren't playing well, and that kind of cleared the air. It showed we were serious about getting something done this season."

Roger the Dodger

Leading up to the first interleague series between the Giants and the Yankees, June 7-9, in New York, Roger Clemens was asked about facing Barry Bonds. The Rocket said he would "introduce myself pretty quick. That big old piece of plastic he has on his elbow, we will see if we can make him take that off and make it even."

Clemens started the series finale and walked Bonds in the opening inning. In the third, he fulfilled his prophecy when a 0-1 pitch struck Bonds on the protective pad. Clemens walked Bonds the next two times while posting a 4-2 victory.

Bonds wouldn't elaborate on the incident, but manager Dusty Baker had plenty to say afterward, angered that Clemens wasn't disciplined.

"It's hard to say it's an accident when he says he's going to do it," Baker said. "I've got a lot of respect for Roger as a pitcher, but if he was in the National League, he might not be known as … what's his nickname, Rocket? Maybe it'd be Roger the dodger.

"You can be bold in the American League and get away with that stuff. It would be a little different in our league. You have to hit."

The Postseason
A History of Frustration:

Even an Earthquake Rained on the Parade

Should He Have Sent Him

It's been more than 40 years since the 1962 World Series, and people recall the bottom of the ninth inning at Candlestick Park as if had happened yesterday. With the series tied 3-3, the mighty New York Yankees were clinging to a 1-0 lead when Ralph Terry took the mound in search of three more outs.

A crowd of 43,948 had its hopes raised when pinch hitter Matty Alou led off with a drag bunt to the right side and was on first with a single. Terry added to the fans' tension by striking out Felipe Alou and Chuck Hiller after they failed to sacrifice. Willie Mays then lined an outside pitch toward the right field corner.

The ball was slowed by the rain-soaked turf and right fielder Roger Maris gracefully made a smooth pickup near the line before the ball could scoot into the corner. With Alou steaming around the bases, third base coach Whitey Lockman quickly considered Maris's arm and Willie McCovey in the on-deck circle.

Lockman prudently held Alou at third base, providing ammunition for the second-guessers when McCovey's liner to second baseman Bobby Richardson ended the game and a World Series which was to be the Giants' last in 27 years! The lack of October success merely placed more emphasis on Lockman's decision, generally regarded as the proper one.

"Wouldn't that have been a helluva way to end the season?" Giants catcher Ed Bailey wondered. "Willie McCovey coming up and the tying run thrown out at the plate by 15 feet? Crazy, man!"

Lockman on his decision: "When the ball hit out there, it didn't scoot like it would on a hard field. It just kind of died, bounced once or twice and rolled to a stop. Maris picks up the ball and throws to the relay man, Richardson.

"That's when I made my judgment not to send Matty, because it was a good throw. If the first throw had been a poor one, I would have sent him, taking a chance that Richardson would not have been able to handle it cleanly."

McCovey Just Misses

The Giants never came closer to winning the World Series in their San Francisco history. They botched Game 6 in 2002, denying them ultimate triumph, and were shaken by an earthquake and the A's in 1989, but it came down to inches in 1962.

Game 7 at Candlestick Park, Oct. 16, pitted Jack Sanford against Ralph Terry, and an anxious crowd of 43,948 assembled for the pitchers' duel. The Yankees entered the bottom of the ninth clinging to a 1-0 lead, their lone run scoring on a double play.

There were two outs and runners on second and third when the Yankees elected to pitch to McCovey instead of loading the bases and facing Orlando Cepeda. Terry defied the percentages and decided to go after the left-handed slugger.

In one of the most famous at-bats in Giants history, McCovey sent a shudder through the crowd with a deep foul to right. The next pitch turned into a screaming liner that second baseman Richardson, stationed perfectly, caught for the final antagonizing out.

"One foot higher, or either way, I guess I would have been a hero," McCovey wistfully recalled many years later. "I hit the ball as hard as I could and I thought I had a hit, but it was right at him. Nothing I could do about that."

Juan Marichal's recollection: "Richardson just got in the way of it. To this day, I won't say he caught the ball; the ball caught him. The force of it drove him to his knees, but he held onto it, and the World Series was over."

The Other Foot

Darryl Spencer experienced excruciating playoff losses from both dugouts. He was with the 1959 Giants when they squandered a two-game lead with eight to go, and he was with the Dodgers when the Giants caught them on the final day—wiping out a three-game lead with six left—and won a three-game playoff in 1962.

From the Dodgers' perspective, Game 3 of that playoff was as devastating as Bobby Thomson's homer in 1951. Why? Because they entered the ninth inning at Dodger Stadium with a 4-2 lead and were baffled by two moves manager Walter Alston made that aided the Giants' cause.

One was replacing second baseman Jim Gilliam with rookie Larry Burright, who botched a play when he was shifted out of position by the manager. The other was not using Don Drysdale or Sandy Koufax in relief in the ninth inning because Alston prematurely was thinking about the World Series, which began the next day.

"That dumb Alston brings in Stan Williams, the wildest man in the league, and he walks [Jim] Davenport to force in the tying run in the ninth inning," Spencer said with disgust many years later. "It was a catastrophe.

"I thought, 'Oh, my God!' Drysdale would have pitched. Koufax would have pitched. We're down to the last inning—who cares about who's going to start the first game of the World Series? What a disaster. So close, just so close."

Giants pitcher Billy O'Dell concurred, adding: "Going into the ninth, we were like dead folks. But then guys got on base and everybody was excited, whooping it up. I think all the hollering contributed to Williams's wildness. It was a shot in the arm when he came out of the bullpen. We expected Drysdale or Koufax. Biggest surprise I ever had."

Spencer, in fact, was so despondent following the loss that he swigged a fifth of bourbon and was on the clubhouse floor, shouting, "Who moved Burright? How can you move Burright?" Spencer was released the following season.

But several Dodgers called that final playoff defeat the most devastating and disappointing loss of their careers. Drysdale summed up: "I'll never forget the scene in the clubhouse. It was like someone had thrown three hand grenades in there. It was the worst I've ever seen."

What, Me Worry?

Following their exhausting playoff victory in Los Angeles, the Giants had to open the World Series against the well-rested Yankees at Candlestick Park the next day. A weary Willie Mays sat motionless in front of his clubhouse cubicle hours before Game 1.

"Willie, are you as tense before this game as you were before the 1951 and 1954 World Series?" a reporter asked.

"Man, after that playoff in L.A., I'm all out of tense," he replied.

It Took Sanford's Finest

The San Francisco Giants posted their first World Series victory, and it took the finest performance in Jack Sanford's career to do it. The grizzled right-hander shackled the Yankees on three hits, posting a 2-0 victory that squared the World Series at one game apiece.

Ralph Terry, who was to gain his revenge in two other matchups with Sanford, fell behind in the first inning on Hiller's leadoff double to right, Felipe Alou's sacrifice and Matty Alou's grounder to second baseman Bobby Richardson.

Manager Alvin Dark also had a good day. He utilized a radical shift on Maris, who was hitless in three at-bats. And he replaced Orlando Cepeda at first base with Willie McCovey, who hit a 400-foot homer to right in the seventh.

"I've never seen anyone hit a ball like that," Terry said, pointing to a spot a few inches below his knees. "It was low and inside, just where I wanted it. He just golfed it out of sight."

Sanford, fighting a cold, summed up: "That lineup scared me from top to bottom, and I was so nervous down the stretch, I couldn't keep my hands still. I wasn't getting the low strikes, so I tried mainly to keep my fastball to the outside."

Hiller's Shining Moment

As is the case in many World Series, lesser players steal the thunder from superstars, partly because they're not the focus of the opposition. Such was certainly the case for Giants second baseman Chuck Hiller in Game 4 of the 1962 World Series.

Hiller enjoyed a career year that season, playing 161 games and batting .276 with 94 runs scored, but his moment of glory came at Yankee Stadium, Oct. 8, with 66,607 in the stands and the Giants trailing two games to one.

In the top of the fifth, with the Giants leading 2-0, Hiller was up with the bases loaded against Marshall Bridges. The count reached 3-2, and Bridges fired a sweeping sidearm curveball that Hiller swung at and missed.

But Hiller, thankfully, had another chance. It was the seventh inning and the bases again were bulging with Giants. Bridges was still pitching, but this time he stayed with his fastball and Hiller parked one over the fence for the first World Series grand slam by a National Leaguer. Best of all, it produced a 7-3 victory, assuring a return to Candlestick.

"I hit that ball and ran like hell," said Hiller, who used pitcher Billy Pierce's bat. "I was sure it was a home run. It felt so good. It wasn't that the bases were loaded. It was just a thrill that it would put us in the lead.

"I hit three home runs in 602 times up that season, and to be able to do that when all those super hitters were playing? A Punch and Judy like me, and do that? It made me feel real good."

Rain Rain Go Away

When Game 5 was delayed by rain, Californians insisted it couldn't happen when the scene shifted to San Francisco. They were wrong. A huge Pacific storm wreaked havoc on the World Series, causing a three-day delay prior to Game 6 and forcing both teams to stage workouts at the drier valley town of Modesto.

Helicopters were used to improve conditions at soggy Candlestick Park, where well-rested pitchers seemed to have an advantage over rusty hitters. Pierce seized the opportunity to continue his home-field mastery, improving to 13-0 at Candlestick with a three-hit, 5-2 triumph over Ford before 43,948.

Hitless in 12 World Series at-bats, Cepeda was rejuvenated by the rest and responded with three hits to pace the win. Pierce received all the support he required in a three-run fourth. Felipe Alou's single and Mays's walk got things going, and an errant pickoff throw by Ford scored the first run.

Cepeda's double and Jim Davenport's single made it 3-0. Maris homered in the fifth, but the Giants answered with two in the bottom half on Harvey Kuenn's first series hit, Hiller's single and run-scoring singles by Felipe Alou and Cepeda.

"I guess this has to be the biggest day of my life," Pierce said. "The whole season has been a great one for me because a lot of people might have thought I was washed up when the White Sox traded me to the Giants. I hope I have proved they were wrong."

A Long Wait

Following their 1962 success, the power-packed Giants thought they'd make several trips to the postseason, but they had to wait until 1971 to do it as the National League Western Division champions. And because they'd clobbered the Pittsburgh Pirates in nine of 12 games during the season, they also figured to reach the World Series.

It certainly looked that way when Gaylord Perry went the distance and Willie McCovey and Tito Fuentes contributed home runs to a 5-4 Game 1 victory at Candlestick Park, but the Bucs had other plans.

Gaining an edge because Juan Marichal had to work the regular-season finale, the Pirates won the next three games in the best-of-five series behind Bob Robertson. Willie Stargell was held hit-less in the series, but Robertson hit three homers in a 9-4 Game 2 romp and added one more in a 2-1 victory over Marichal in Game 3.

The Giants took a 5-2 lead in the second inning of Game 4 at Three Rivers Stadium with the help of homers by Chris Speier and McCovey, but shutout relief by Bruce Kison and Dave Giusti and three RBI each by Roberto Clemente, Al Oliver and Richie Hebner prevailed 9-5 in the finale.

Dravecky Delivers

A 5-3 victory by the host St. Louis Cardinals in the 1987 NLCS opener temporary blunted the Giants' impetus, but the old adage that "momentum is as good as next day's pitcher" never rang truer when left-hander Dave Dravecky took the mound at Busch Stadium, Oct. 7.

A record crowd of 55,331 jammed Busch for the second straight day, but had little to cheer as Dravecky pitched his finest major-league game. The baffled Cardinals mustered singles by Tom Herr and Jim Lindeman and nothing more in a 5-0 victory powered by Jeff Leonard and Will Clark homers.

"No question, this was by far the best game I ever pitched," Dravecky said. "I think it's obvious that if you keep their speed off the bases, that's a major part of it. The key is not to let the baserunners take the emphasis off the hitters."

Dravecky didn't yield a hit after Herr singled in the fourth, facing the minimum 18 batters the rest of the way while aided by two double plays. His lone two-on threat was in the fourth, when Ozzie Smith led off with a walk and Herr singled to center. But Terry Pendelton, Willie McGee and Lindeman all flied out, strand-ing the runners.

Krukow's Finest Hour

Mike Krukow regarded winning his 20th game in 1986 as a career highlight, but that all changed before 57,997 at Candlestick Park, Oct. 10, 1987. The NLCS had shifted to San Francisco, where the Cardinals took the series with a 6-5 victory in Game 3, so all eyes were on Krukow in his Game 4 matchup with Danny Cox.

He admittedly was nervous, and it showed when successive one-out singles by Curt Ford, Tony Pena, Cox and Vince Coleman gave the Cardinals a 2-0 lead in the second. Ozzie Smith then lined into a double play and Krukow held them scoreless on five singles the rest of the way.

"In 1986, winning 20 was a personal thing, statistics on the back of a baseball card," Krukow said following his 4-2 victory. "Here, we've got a chance to be a part of baseball history."

Robby Thompson's solo homer in the fourth started the Giants' comeback, and they went ahead to stay on Kevin Mitchell's two-out double and Jeffrey Leonard's record fourth homer in four games in the fifth inning.

But it was Thompson's fielding that saved the day. With two on and one out in the Cardinals' two-run second, the second baseman speared Smith's liner and doubled Coleman off first.

"It was a red alert in the bullpen," Krukow recalled. "There were sparks coming from out there. That was a great play by Robby. It gave me a chance to regroup. That catch was the turning point."

The Price Is Right

The Cardinals finally figured out how to stop Leonard, but they had no answers for reliever Joe Price on Oct. 11, when a record crowd of 59,363 showed up at Candlestick Park to watch the Giants inch closer to their first pennant in 25 years.

Each team scored single runs in the first and third innings of Game 5, and the Cardinals took a 3-2 lead off Rick Reuschel in the third on Terry Pendleton's two-out triple and an error by Will Clark.

The Giants erupted with four runs off Greg Mathews in the bottom of the fourth on Jose Uribe's two-run single, pinch hitter

Mike Aldrete's sacrifice fly and Robby Thompson's run-scoring triple for a 6-3 lead.

They just needed to hold the Cardinals for a 3-2 edge in the best-of-seven series, and Price, who was demoted to Triple-A during the season, was the right man for the job. He yielded but one hit and one walk in five shutout innings, placing St. Louis on the brink of elimination.

"I feel great; it feels very satisfying," the six-foot-four Price said after striking out six. "I'm just going to relax and enjoy the flight to St. Louis. I've been around long enough to know things can change in a hurry."

Cardinals and Cowbells

When the Giants returned to St. Louis, needing one win in two games for the pennant, they were greeted by raucous fans agitated by Jeffrey Leonard's flaps-down home run trot and Chili Davis's "cowtown" reference. So, 55,331—some bringing cowbells—packed Busch Stadium for Game 6, a rematch of Dave Dravecky and John Tudor in Game 2.

Dravecky was nearly as dominant this time, yielding but one run in six innings, but that tainted tally was his downfall in a 1-0 defeat that squared the series. Right fielder Candy Maldonado and the Busch lighting could be blamed for this one.

Geronimo Pena led off the second inning with a sinking liner to right. Maldonado lost it in the glare of the lights and slid under the ball, which nearly hit him in the head. It went for a triple, and Jose Oquendo's one-out sacrifice fly to short right scored the game's lone run when Maldonado threw poorly.

"I saw the ball coming off the bat, and then I lost it in the lights," a downcast Maldonado explained. "I felt it hit my arm. I wish it would have hit me in the chest and stayed in front of me."

The Giants had two excellent opportunities to score. Clark's one-out walk and Bob Melvin's single threatened in the second, but Willie McGee's great catch of Jose Uribe's liner to center and Dravecky's grounder snuffed that threat.

In the fifth, Melvin and Uribe opened with singles. Dravecky bunted and Melvin was thrown out on a controversial play at third base. Robby Thompson and Kevin Mitchell followed with flies to center and the shutout was preserved.

Deflated and Defeated

The Game 6 loss took the swagger out of the Giants, and Danny Cox capitalized with an eight-hit shutout and a 6-0 victory that thrust the Cardinals into the World Series before 55,331 taunting and happy fans.

It ended rather quickly. The Cardinals scored four runs in the second inning on successive one-out singles by Terry Pendleton, Geronimo Pena and Willie McGee followed by Jose Oquendo's three-run homer off Atlee Hammaker. Tom Herr's two-run single in the sixth capped the scoring.

"The home run was the turning point," manager Roger Craig said of Oquendo's third career blast in 914 at-bats. "We have nothing to be ashamed of. You have to credit their pitching staff. No runs in two games. They were great."

The Giants, in fact, were scoreless in the final 22 innings of the NLCS, and what made it worse, according to Mike Krukow, was "having to sit in our hotel rooms across from the ballpark all night and hearing the Cardinals fan celebrate. That was brutal."

The Thrill Takes Over

The 1989 season was one of Will Clark's finest, yet he was overshadowed by MVP teammate Kevin Mitchell as the Giants won their second division title in three years. But when the NLCS opened at Wrigley Field, it was The Thrill's turn to shine.

Playing before 39,195 in the "cozy confines," Clark enjoyed the greatest batting performance in San Francisco playoff history, almost single-handedly demolishing the Chicago Cubs with four hits, including two home runs and six RBI off Greg Maddux, in an 11-3 Game 1 romp, Oct. 4.

"He had one helluva week," Cubs manager Don Zimmer declared after Clark reached base all five times and outscored Chicago 4-3. Mitchell contributed a three-run homer and each Giants starter with the exception of pitcher Scott Garrelts hit safely.

Brett Butler's leadoff single, a sacrifice and Clark's double to center gave the Giants the lead in the first inning. After Mitchell singled, Matt Williams's two-run double made it 3-0, but the Cubs rallied on Ryne Sandberg's double and Mark Grace's homer in the bottom half.

Clark and Sandberg each homered in the third, leaving the Giants with a 4-3 lead before Clark sealed the deal in the fourth. Pat Sheridan and Jose Uribe opened with singles and Butler was walked intentionally after Uribe stole second, loading the bases with one out.

Not for long. After Thompson popped out, Clark dramatically delivered a 400-foot grand slam homer over the right field wall for a sudden 8-3. Garrelts worked seven strong innings, striking out six and walking one. Jeff Brantley and Atlee Hammaker mopped up.

"You really can't explain it," Clark said of his binge, which included the first NLCS grand slam since Giants batting coach Dusty Baker connected for the Dodgers in 1977. "This definitely could be a momentum builder for us."

Will vs. the Wild Thing

It was a warm, 78-degree day at Candlestick Park, where a record 62,804 sat in anticipation of a pennant celebration. Will Clark once again didn't disappoint, providing one of the most dramatic hits in Giants history.

Kevin Mitchell's error in left field and Ryne Sandberg's double gave the Cubs an unearned run off Rick Reuschel in the third, and Mike Bielecki had the Giants blanked until Clark's triple and Mitchell's sacrifice fly made it 1-1 in the seventh.

Bielecki had a three-hitter and two outs in the bottom of the eighth when he suddenly lost his control. Pinch hitter Candy

Maldonado walked, and so did Brett Butler and Robby Thompson, loading the bases for you-know-who.

Zimmer summoned Mitch "The Wild Thing" Williams, and the Cubs' closer quickly got ahead of Clark 0-2. After ball one, Clark fouled off two pitches before drilling a searing grounder to center for a two-run single and a 3-1 lead.

The fans were jumping with joy, especially after Steve Bedrosian retired the first two batters in the ninth. But pinch hitters Rick Wilkins, Mitch Webster and Jerome Walton singled in succession to bring the Cubs within one at 3-2 before Sandberg's groundout to second sent the Giants to the World Series for the first time in 27 years.

"You can talk all you want about big-game performers like Joe Montana and Michael Jordan, but it doesn't get any better than what Will did under extreme pressure," Craig said. "The bases were loaded, he had two strikes on him and he was facing a sidewinding left-hander who throws 95 mph. It was amazing to see."

Clark, who finished with NLCS records for batting average (.650), hits (13), runs (eight), extra-base hits (six), total bases (26) and slugging percentage (1.200), summed up: "The ball is looking real big right now."

All Shook Up

Whenever the Giants landed on the national stage, the natural elements seemed to become a factor. In the 1961 All-Star Game, for instance, a gust of wind that caused Stu Miller's balk gave Candlestick Park more notoriety. One year later, an unseasonal storm wreaked havoc with the field and caused a lengthy rain delay.

When the 1989 World Series shifted to Candlestick Park, Oct. 17, it was more of the same, and on a much larger scale. It was 5:04 p.m., and 60,000 fans were settling in their seats when a rumble shook the stadium. Seasoned Californians knew immediately that it was an earthquake, but nobody imagined its magnitude.

In fact, when the shaking stopped, most fans expected Game 3 to begin as scheduled. Not until a collapsed section on the upper deck of the Bay Bridge was shown on the huge videoscreen did people begin to realize the devastation wrought by the quake, which registered 7.1 on the Richter Scale.

When the damage was surveyed, including a flattened portion of the Cypress freeway in Oakland, baseball seemed so irrelevant. There were 67 deaths attributed to the disaster, but baseball was credited with saving many lives because so many commuters already were at the ballpark or watching TV at home.

"At this moment, it would be inappropriate to play baseball," said commissioner Fay Vincent, announcing the delay the next day. "Baseball's priority obviously is a very limited one: To finish the World Series in a graceful way. Our highest priority is the safety of the citizens and a sensitivity to the dignity of the community."

A Forgettable Sweep

When Game 3 was rescheduled for Oct. 27, a delay of 10 days, the World Series practically was anticlimactic. Minds were on the earthquake's aftermath and it was difficult for the fans and the players to totally concentrate on baseball, as Giants catcher Terry Kennedy astutely observed.

"It might not be a real sharp series from a performance standpoint," he predicted. "We can get back into it physically once the games start, but mentally and psychologically it will be impossible to get it back to where it was."

Kennedy's assessment was accurate. The next two games at Candlestick resembled the spring training variety. But that didn't prevent the A's from posting the first World Series sweep since 1966 with sloppy 13-7 and 9-6 victories behind Dave Stewart and Mike Moore, who were effective enough to each post their second wins.

A crowd of 62,038 assembled for Game 3, and Dave Henderson's two-run double and a pair of solo homers helped to forge an 8-3 lead after five innings. Jose Canseco belted a three-run homer for Oakland, and the Giants made it more respectable with a four-run ninth featuring pinch hitter Bill Bathe's three-run homer.

In the clincher, before 62,032 on Oct. 28, Rickey Henderson's leadoff homer, triple and single helped to forge an 8-0 lead before the Giants crept back. Two-run homers by Kevin Mitchell and Greg Litton helped the home club score six of the last seven runs—too little, too late.

"The A's were just too powerful," Giants general manager Al Rosen said. "The tragedy of that World Series is all the people who lost their lives and the damage to the infrastructure of the cities. I really remember more about that than I do about the games."

Devon Not Just Grand

While the Giants relentlessly were dashing toward a division title, closer Rod Beck called it "a team of Dustiny," a tribute to Dusty Baker's leadership. Unfortunately, it was the Marlins who were a team of destiny, sweeping the Giants en route to a pennant and a World Series championship before the ballclub suddenly was torn apart.

The clincher came before 57,188 at Candlestick Park, Oct. 3, a date synonymous with Giants playoff success (Bobby Thomson, 1962, etc.). Devon White's sixth-inning grand slam homer off Wilson Alvarez powered a clinching 6-2 victory.

"The Florida Marlins played better than we did for three given days," summed up Jeff Kent, who accounted for the S.F. scoring with two solo homers off Alex Fernandez. "It's tough. I still don't feel like it's over. But we've just got to turn the page. It's over."

Kent's first homer staked Alvarez to a 1-0 lead in the fourth before the Marlins rallied with two outs and none on in the sixth. Singles by Moises Alou and Jeff Conine followed by Charles Johnson's walk loaded the bases for White, who drove a 2-1 pitch to left for the cruncher.

"We wanted to play a lot longer than this—it seemed whatever they needed they got," Baker said. "I would have preferred a 2-2-1 setup where you'd play the first two games at your place, but there's nothing you can do about it."

The first-round playoff soon was altered just as Baker envisioned, but it proved too little too late—even when the Giants returned to the playoffs three years later.

The Livan Is Easy

Something had to give as the Giants engaged the New York Mets in the 2000 Division Series opener when Livan Hernandez, a pitcher who had never lost a postseason game, was opposed by Mike Hampton, who had never lost to San Francisco. A crowd of 40,930 jammed Pacific Bell Park, Oct. 4, to find out the answer.

The Giants, fueled by a 23-9 stretch drive, and Hernandez didn't disappoint. He improved to 5-0 with a 2.75 ERA in postseason games by shackling the Mets 5-1 in Game 1 of the NLDS. The Cuban right-hander limited New York to five hits and one run in seven and two-thirds innings.

"When he's throwing strikes, you get on the back of the bus and ride it because Livan is driving," Jeff Kent said after contributing a single and a run-scoring grounder off Hampton, who lost after going 9-0 against the Giants in regular-season games.

Added Hernandez, MVP of the NLCS and the World Series with the 1997 Florida Marlins: "I don't know why I do so good in the playoffs. I felt the same, but being in the playoffs is special. When you get here, you have to play hard because you have a chance to go to the World Series."

It was 1-1 and Hampton had two outs and nobody on base in the third inning when the Giants had their fans waving rally towels with a four-run uprising that started with Bill Mueller's single and Barry Bonds's tie-breaking triple. After Kent walked, Ellis Burks delivered a three-run homer to left.

A Snow Flurry

J. T. Snow smashed the first truly dramatic home run in Pacific Bell Park history, but his elation over a game-tying three-run blast in the ninth inning of Game 2 in the 2000 NLDS cruelly was short-lived. That's because former teammate Darryl Hamilton stole the show in the 10th inning and helped the Mets to a series-squaring 5-4 victory on Oct.5.

Al Leiter had a four-hitter and a 4-1 lead entering the bottom of the ninth—thanks to Edgardo Alfonzo's two-run homer off Felix Rodriguez in the top half, when 40,430 partisans finally had something to cheer. After Barry Bonds led off with a double, closer Armando Benitez replaced Leiter and Jeff Kent hit an infield single.

With one out, Snow turned on some inside heat and hit a towering homer that hugged the right field line and dropped into the first row of arcade seats for a sudden 4-4. With two outs and none on in the 10th, Hamilton quickly stole the momentum with a pinch double before scoring on Jay Payton's single off Rodriguez.

"It was exciting—the emotion, the fans and all that—but I'd trade all of it for a win," Snow said of his first homer and RBI as a pinch hitter. "There was kind of an emotional swing with that at-bat, but they took it away. Give them credit."

Hawaiian Punch

"It ain't over—this club plays best with its back to the wall," Jeff Kent insisted after the NLDS shifted to Shea Stadium and the Giants once again suffered a painful extra-inning defeat. This time it was Benny Agbayani's 13th-inning homer that drove a stake through their hearts, producing a walkoff, 3-2 victory for the New York Mets on Oct. 7.

Agbayani's bomb off Aaron Fultz gave the Mets a 2-1 lead in the best-of-five series as starter Rick Reed and their bullpen blanked the Giants over the final nine innings. A crowd of 56,270 sat through a tension-filled five-hour, 22-minute game that left the weary Giants wondering what happened to their vaunted offense.

Four of their 11 hits were bunched in a two-run fourth, and that was it. Russ Ortiz lost a no-hitter in the sixth when Mike Bordick walked and pinch hitter Darryl Hamilton and Timo Perez followed with singles with no outs. Ortiz and Alan Embree worked out of further trouble, but Edgardo Alfonzo doubled off Robb Nen in the eighth for a 2-2 tie.

Both teams threatened in extra innings as bullpens squirmed out of trouble. But with one out in the bottom of the 13th, Agbayani sent a fat 1-0 fastball soaring majestically to center for a 385-foot homer. The crowd chanted, "Benny! Benny!" and the scoreboard flashed "Hawaiian Punch" in tribute to his heritage while he was mobbed at the plate.

"That's what baseball is all about," Dusty Baker said following the stirring finish. "Anybody who turned the TV off doesn't like baseball or has no emotions. We've won two in a row before. This thing isn't over, but they're [Mets] acting like it is."

Down and Out

The wild-card Mets moved in for the kill on Oct. 8, and 56,245 jammed into Shea Stadium to watch the Giants succumb meekly. Right-hander Bobby Jones's career-best one-hitter extended San Francisco's scoreless streak to 18 innings in a 4-0 victory that boosted New York to the NLCS and an eventual date in the Subway World Series.

Unlike the two extra-inning victories that preceded it, Game 4 was devoid of drama as Jones left the Giants perplexed. He retired the first 12 batters and the final 13, in between yielding a leadoff double to Jeff Kent in the fifth inning, a drive that grazed third baseman Robin Ventura's glove.

Ventura's two-run homer off Mark Gardner in the first inning and Edgardo Alfonzo's two-run double off him in the fifth accounted for all the scoring. Both scoring bursts came after two outs and none on, and manager Dusty Baker was criticized for allowing Gardner to bat in the top of the fifth when the Giants posed their only threat.

After Kent doubled on a 1-2 pitch, Ellis Burks sent him to third with a warning-track shot to right. J. T. Snow walked and Rich Aurilia flied to short left. Doug Mirabelli walked, loading the bases. With a tired bullpen, Baker stayed with Gardner, and he popped to second in the Giants' last gasp.

"I thought we'd have more opportunities," said Baker, who had nobody warming up in the bullpen. Summed up Barry Bonds: "We were ready, and then Ventura kicked us in the stomach and Alfonzo took the wind out of us. They just played better than we did."

A Perfect Start

The Giants had merely one playoff victory in 13 years when they entered Turner Field for the opener of the NL Division Series, Oct. 2, 2002. Confidence ran high because of an eight-game winning streak, yet nobody imagined what would transpire before 41,903 disbelieving Atlanta Braves fans.

Left-hander Tom Glavine was treated like a batting practice pitcher —10 hits and six runs in five innings—and the Giants rolled to an 8-5 victory behind Russ Ortiz's seven strong innings and a 12-hit attack featuring Benito Santiago.

"If anyone had told me the Giants would have eight runs without Bonds or Kent driving in one, I'd have thought they were crazy," Glavine said. Added manager Dusty Baker: "It just turned out to be our day."

The Giants never trailed after J. T. Snow's two-run double and David Bell's single created a 3-0 lead in the top of the second. Rich Aurilia's two-run double crowned a three-run fourth and Santiago added a two-run double in the sixth off Chris Hammond, who hadn't yielded a run in 32 games since June 30.

The Giants' day, indeed.

Backed to the Wall

After Kirk Rueter emulated fellow lefty Tom Glavine and was rocked by the host Braves 7-3 in Game 2, returning to Pacific Bell Park provided some comfort for the Giants, who promptly lost their home-field advantage when reliever Manny Aybar became the goat of Game 3 before 43,043 fans.

Aybar tied the major-league record with five runs on two pitches after Jason Schmidt and Greg Maddux battled to a 1-1 tie after five innings. With one out in the sixth, Schmidt walked the bases loaded, and Dusty Baker summoned Aybar. Boom! Vinny Castilla lined a first-pitch slider to left for a two-run single.

Keith Lockhart saw a fat fastball on the very next pitch, blasting it into the arcade seats in right field for a three-run homer and 6-1. The Braves' 10-2 rout placed the Giants on the brink of elimination in the best-of-five series, and it was up to Livan Hernandez to live up to his postseason reputation and keep the Giants alive in Game 4.

Not a problem. Hernandez, improving to 6-0 in the postseason, held the Braves hitless over the first four innings. And the Giants once again obliterated Glavine in what would be his final Atlanta start, bolting to a 7-0 lead after three innings and cruising to a series-squaring 8-3 victory before 43,070 at Pac Bell.

The clutch performance, which included a three-run homer and four RBI from Rich Aurilia and three RBI by Benito Santiago, had the Giants send 20 batters to the plate against Glavine in two and two-thirds innings. Seven hit safely, five others walked, and there were three sacrifices. Aurilia had three of those hits.

"Livan was very focused today," Baker said. "He knew we needed it, and he enhanced his reputation as a big-game pitcher. He was throwing the ball hard, and he was sharp, really sharp. And it helped that we got some runs early."

Chopping the Braves

An all-night flight and the Atlanta Braves couldn't deter the Giants' 2002 charge in the playoffs. The odds seemed to favor the perennial champions when the NLDS returned to Turner Field for Game 5, Oct. 7, and a tomahawk-chopping crowd of 45,203 showed up for the celebration.

Instead, longtime adversary Barry Bonds homered and scored twice, Kenny Lofton provided the winning run, Robb Nen enjoyed his redemption, and Russ Ortiz became the first Giants pitcher in 69 years to win twice in a postseason series. It all added up to a 3-2 victory and a trip to the World Series.

Shortly after arriving at the ballpark, shortstop Rich Aurilia had a premonition that Bonds would have a big night to change his mostly negative playoff fortunes, telling reporters: "We look forward to him going out and having a big game for us, just like we do every game."

As if on cue, Bonds got the Giants' offense going with a sharp single to left off Kevin Millwood leading off the second. He advanced on Benito Santiago's grounder and scored on Reggie Sanders's two-out single to center, triggering the club's first victory in a postseason series that went the distance since 1921.

Bonds made it 2-0 with a leadoff homer in the fourth, and it was 3-1 in the seventh on J. T. Snow's double, a pair of walks and Lofton's fly. Ortiz, who would be traded to the Braves two months later, worked into the sixth, yielding one run, and Nen got even with Chipper Jones in the ninth.

On Aug. 15 on the same field, Nen squandered a 3-1 lead in the ninth inning on Jones's two-out, two-strike, two-run single in a game that went into the books as a 3-3 tie following a two-hour, 33-minute rain delay. This time, with one run in and a runner on with no outs, Nen struck out Gary Sheffield and retired Jones on a series-ending double play.

The end of years of frustration erupted in delirium and dancing, with Livan Hernandez leading the way. Manny Aybar, Pedro Feliz and Yorvit Torrealba joined the impromptu clubhouse merengue while jubilant teammates cheered them on. The Giants were past the first round for the first time since 1989.

Lofton Fires 'Em Up

Kenny Lofton was acquired in July to light a spark under the Giants' offense in the leadoff spot. What he did in Game 1 of the 2002 NLCS with the St. Louis Cardinals set the tone before 52,175 in Game 1 at Busch Stadium, Oct. 9.

He opened the game with a walk and scored the first run on Benito Santiago's two-out single. His two-out single ignited a four-run second in which he scored on Barry Bonds's two-run triple. And his two-out homer built a 6-1 lead off Mike Morris in the third.

The Cardinals, stunned by the turn of events and aggravated by Lofton admiring his home run, sent a message when he came to bat in the fifth. Mike Crudale brushed him back with a high inside pitch, Lofton yelled at him, and both benches emptied.

Managers Dusty Baker and Tony La Russa came close to having at each other. When order was restored, Santiago's two-run homer contributed to a 9-6 victory, but it was Lofton who fired up both teams.

Curiously, Lofton was hitless in his next 16 NLCS at-bats, but he finished the series just like he started it—with three straight hits in his final three at-bats, including the game-winning single in the ninth inning of the Game 5 clincher.

"I just happened to be there—it all comes down to opportunity," a giddy Lofton said of his big hit. "It's the biggest hit of my career, and I was happy because I knew we were going to the World Series. I just kept my focus."

Benito's Big Bomb

St. Louis Cardinals manager Tony La Russa wanted no part of Barry Bonds, and Benito Santiago made him pay with the biggest hit of the Giants' postseason. In fact, Santiago's tie-breaking two-run homer off Rick White in the eighth inning might have been the Giants' most significant home run in 51 years— since Bobby Thomson's "Shot Heard 'Round the World" to clinch the 1951 pennant.

Benito Santiago won NLCS MVP honors in 2002 and made the Cardinals pay for walking Barry Bonds to get to him in Game 4 of the NLCS. Santiago hit a tie-breaking two-run homer in the eighth inning to give the Giants a 3-1 lead. (Photo courtesy of the San Francisco Giants)

With two out and none on, La Russa ordered the right-handed White to walk Bonds intentionally. Santiago then hammered a 3-2 pitch into the left field seats, and the Giants held on for a 4-3 victory in Game 4 to take a 3-1 lead in the NLCS before 42,676 admirers at Pacific Bell Park.

"Along with Brian Johnson's homer against the Dodgers [1997] and J. T. Snow's playoff homer against the Mets [2000], I can't think of any bigger homers since I've been managing," Dusty Baker said. "It was huge."

A delirious Santiago agreed wholeheartedly, adding: "It was unbelievable, a dream come true. When I hit the ball, I knew I hit it hard. The time before that he struck me out on the same pitch [an inside fastball]. I tried to put the good side of the bat on the ball, and it happened."

Thanks for Coming

There's no question the Giants had an unusual season in 2002, coming from nowhere to land in the World Series. And how it happened also was curious, because the three players who collaborated on defeating the St. Louis Cardinals in the NLCS clincher—David Bell, Shawon Dunston and Kenny Lofton—wouldn't be back in 2003.

A perfectly scripted two-out rally in the bottom of the ninth inning, Oct. 14, created an improbable finish for 42,673 fans and captured the Giants' third pennant in 45 S.F. seasons. They strung together consecutive two-out line drive singles to center by Bell, Dunston and Lofton for a 2-1 victory, setting off fireworks and a wild celebration at Pacific Bell Park.

With two down in the ninth, Bell smacked a first-pitch single off starter Matt Morris. Dunston followed with a single, and Lofton hit reliever Steve Kline's first pitch and jumped for joy at first base. It looked like extra innings before Bell's single produced a team-leading .412 average in the series.

Then Dunston, a 39-year-old remnant dormant much of the season, kept the rally alive. He was so choked up afterward that he had difficulty speaking. "This is Barry Bonds's team, and Jeff Kent's team, but we're all part of it," he said. "It was a tough year for me, but it's my best year because I'm going to the World Series. I'm finally going."

While Dunston was sentimental, teammates were soaking up champagne and the giddy atmosphere surrounding a team entering the World Series with 15 wins in 18 games. "We're playing like a bunch of kids and enjoying it," Rich Aurilia beamed after a .333 series. "There's no pressure. We're relaxed and having fun. It's great to see so many veterans enjoying it."

What a Relief

Barry Bonds's first World Series at-bat appropriately produced a 418-foot home run off Anaheim Angels ace Jarrod Washburn, but the Giants needed hitless relief to nail down a 4-3 Game 1 victory at Edison Field, Oct. 19, 2002. It was their first World Series triumph in 40 years—since Billy Pierce beat the Yankees in Game 6 of 1962.

Reggie Sanders and J. T. Snow also connected for the Giants, neutralizing a pair of solo homers by Troy Glaus before 44,603 in the Angels' first World Series in their 42-season existence. Robb Nen retired the side in the ninth after Felix Rodriguez nailed all four batters he faced and Tim Worrell issued a walk in a hitless eighth.

"Winning the first one is really big," manager Dusty Baker said. "It jump starts you for the series. We've had to win on the road, and we've been a very good road team [5-1] throughout these playoffs. And for Barry to start off like that, it's a good sign. He was really focused and kind of quiet today, and into what he had to do."

The three Giants' homers probably were a shock to an Angels' pitching staff that hadn't been tagged for a postseason homer in 48 innings since Jorge Posada of the Yankees connected in Game 4 of the opening round. Bonds hit a high inside fastball to place the Giants ahead, and Sanders followed with a 390-foot

*J. T. Snow was one of three Giants to go deep in Game 1 of the 2002
World Series, a 4-3 victory over the Anaheim Angels.
(Photo courtesy of the San Francisco Giants)*

shot one out later, taking some pressure off Jason Schmidt, who never trailed.

"Barry's homer was big," Schmidt said. "It was 0-0, and you don't want to give up the first run. His homer started things and got the team fired up. It took some tension off. I had to take care of tickets for the family, but as soon as I got on the mound, it was tunnel vision."

After Bonds and Sanders homered, Glaus blasted an 0-2 Schmidt pitch to left with one out in the bottom half, thereby joining Bonds as the 26th and 27th players in history to do so on their first World Series at-bats. Snow's two-run homer chased Washburn and made it 4-1 in the sixth.

Bell, Bullpen Equal Victory

The adage about good pitching stopping good hitting finally had its practical application in the 2002 World Series just as the vaunted Anaheim offense threatened to make it a runaway. The Angels blew away the Giants 10-4 in Game 3 at Pacific Bell Park and took a 3-0 lead on Troy Glaus's two-run homer in Game 4.

But 42,703 partisans saw what they wanted in Game 4, Oct. 23, when the Giants' pitchers faced the minimum 18 batters over the final six innings and David Bell's tie-breaking eighth-inning single over previously unscathed Francisco Rodriguez produced a series-squaring 4-3 victory.

Kirk Rueter finally settled down after Glaus's third-inning homer and turned the ball over to the bullpen in a 3-3 tie after igniting a three-run fifth with an infield single. Felix Rodriguez retired the side in the seventh, and Tim Worrell had a one-two-three inning in the eighth before Robb Nen registered the save.

Francisco Rodriguez, who was 5-0 in the postseason, breezed through the heart of the Giants' order in the seventh, giving him 12 straight outs in the World Series. Then the Giants stirred in the bottom of the eighth. J. T. Snow lined a single to right. After catcher Bengie Molina's passed ball sent Snow to second, Reggie Sanders fouled out and Bell sharply lined a 1-0 fastball to center for the tie-breaking run.

"I was going to make him throw a strike, and he did on the first pitch," Snow said. "Then he threw a ball, and then I hit a slider. After the passed ball, I was on second, and I knew David would get a hit. He can pretty much hit anybody's fastball, and he did."

Kent's Fond Farewell

It was the Anaheim Angels' balanced offense that commanded the most attention in the early stages of the World Series, but the Giants flexed their muscle before 42,713 well-entertained spectators in Game 5, the last game of the 2002 season at Pacific Bell Park.

NLCS Most Valuable Player Benito Santiago had three RBI as the Giants jumped to a six-run lead after two innings, and Jeff Kent added a pair of two-run homers for four RBI and scored four runs, Oct. 24, in a record-setting 16-4 romp.

"What a great way to end your season in your ballpark," Kent said after what turned out to be his final Giants home game. "It might be my last home game here, but the World Series is more important than my free agency. This game played with my emotions."

Kent's homers and one by Rich Aurilia gave the Giants 12, the most by a National League team in World Series history— and with a bullpen that limited the Angels to one run over the final four and one-third innings before 42,713 thunderstick-clapping fans.

"We're not smelling it yet," cautioned Rich Aurilia after the 16 runs were the second most in World Series history, topped only by the Yankees' 18-4 rout of the Giants in 1936. "We came off the field businesslike. We haven't done anything yet."

How correct he was.

Bursting the Bubble

It all looked so easy when Jeff Kent's run-scoring single in the top of the seventh inning gave the Giants a 5-0 lead in Game

6 at Anaheim, Oct. 26, 2002. After 48 years of frustration, champagne was about to flow in their World Series clubhouse.

The Giants could smell it. Barry Bonds would finally get his ring, and his sixth-inning home run just about cinched World Series MVP honors. Then the Rally Monkey appeared and 44,506 fans went ape along with the resilient Anaheim Angels, who rallied for a stunning 6-5 victory at Edison Field.

Troy Glaus's two-run double off Robb Nen in the eighth erased the Giants' lead and was the winning blow. Scott Spiezio's three-run homer off Felix Rodriguez in the seventh ignited the comeback. Darin Erstad's leadoff homer, Tim Salmon's single and Garret Anderson's bloop double off Tim Worrell preceded Glaus's game-winner.

Home runs by Bonds and Shawon Dunston—the two oldest players on the team—and Russ Ortiz's two-hit shutout for six innings gave the Giants momentum. Then Dusty Baker lifted his starter during the seventh-inning rally and angered some Angels by flipping the ball to Ortiz as a souvenir of an expected victory.

The End of a Dream

In a dazzling World Series that had more twists, turns and thrills than a Disneyland attraction, the final magical carpet ride belonged to the Anaheim Angels. Garret Anderson's three-run triple off Livan Hernandez in the third inning provided the impetus for a 4-1 Game 7 victory at Edison Field, ending the Giants' dream season.

It was a bitter defeat for the Giants, who had a 5-0 lead in the seventh inning of Game 6 before the Angels rallied in the highest-scoring World Series in history. The two clubs combined for 85 runs, three more than the Yankees and Pirates in 1960.

"I never imagined four runs would be enough to win the way this series was going," Dusty Baker said in what would be his final game as Giants manager. "It's a difficult time right now. Your heart is heavy, your stomach is empty."

The players couldn't mask their disappointment, either. Many were teary-eyed and exhausted. Hernandez was bent forward on a clubhouse chair, sobbing uncontrollably while being consoled by pitching coach Dave Righetti.

Barry Bonds was thankful for the experience, yet remained unfulfilled in his pursuit of a championship ring. "You want the results to be different, but what can you do?" Bonds said softly. "Unfortunately, we were on the short end of the stick. The Angels played great. I'm not going to lie. It was fun. I'll go to spring training and try again."

Jeff Kent, who wore a Giants uniform for the last time, said he was holding back his emotions until the drive home up I-5. He conceded that allowing Game 6 to slip away was significant, but refused to call it critical.

"Last night [Game 6] was not the deciding game," Kent said. "We had two games in Anaheim, and we knew we had to win one. You've got to win if you're going to be world champions. You've just got to play, and they outplayed us. It was a frustrating end to a great year, so it's difficult to swallow."

Snow's Save Rates

J. T. Snow compensated for a mediocre 2002 season by batting .333 in the playoffs and World Series, including .407 as the Giants reached the seventh game against the Anaheim Angels. But nobody seems to remember Snow's performance.

Instead, the graceful and quick-thinking first baseman became a national celebrity because he rescued batboy Darren Baker from potential harm with a swooping grab while scoring a run in Game 5.

"Wherever I went this winter, that's all people would talk about," Snow said. "I hit over .400 in the World Series and hit safely in each game, but nobody talked about that. I was a real big hit with moms and kids at the shopping malls. I had no idea it would be such a big deal."

The incident, during the Giants' 16-4 rout at Pacific Bell Park, became a national story partly because it made for a cute photo, but mainly because it raised safety issues. Dusty Baker's son was just three and one-half, so now batboys must be at least 14 to be on the field.

"I think that's too drastic," Snow said. "I think you can have a batboy seven, eight, or nine, as long as you have a 14-year-old as the other guy. My son Shane just turned five and asked me when he could be a batboy. I told him when he's 14, and he started crying."

Willie Mays: The Greatest Giant Ever

San Francisco's Superstar Import
Gradually Gained Acceptance

Willie Who?

Giants fans were slow to accept Willie Mays's greatness when the club first moved to San Francisco. He was identified with the New York years, images that had him playing stickball in the streets and catching Vic Wertz's drive in the 1954 World Series. The new fans were more eager to embrace rookies like Orlando Cepeda and Jim Davenport.

Even the Bay Area press was skeptical. The scribes expected more home runs from Mays, who instead became a hitting machine at Seals Stadium. He belted a career-high 208 hits (still an S.F. record) and batted a career-best .347, but it didn't seem to be enough. His managers knew better.

"Willie Mays is the world's greatest athlete," Bill Rigney declared in 1958. "His motions are so smooth, I even get a kick out of the silky way he puts on his coat. He is the only man I know who can win a game for you in every department of the game, except pitching.

"When I saw him walk into the clubhouse, we had a chance to win. To me, there was nothing he couldn't do. And as ferociously as Jackie Robinson played, Willie played it with a happiness of doing the thing he loved to do best."

Alvin Dark, who was a teammate before he managed Mays in 1962 added: "You can't judge Willie on a single game. You have to judge him on 11 seasons. He does the things that you have to see again and again to recognize that they are the things that Mays does, and not things that just happened."

Willie Mays was the greatest all-around player to ever put on a Giants uniform. (AP/WWP)

Get Out of the Way

Willie Mays was as skillful afield as he was at the plate, and one of his strengths was covering a lot of ground. That came in especially handy when outfielders of inferior ability flanked him. That definitely was the case with Leon Wagner, who retold a story about a day at Wrigley Field in 1959 when he was in left and Willie Kirkland in right.

"Willie told both of us to guard the line," Wagner recalled, "so here's Mays playing practically the entire outfield. Man, he had two blocks to cover! Then Ernie Banks unloads a real blast, and I start going back toward the wall.

"I figure I'm gonna run into the ivy and that the ball is going into the seats. Then I hear footsteps, and here comes Willie. He came running up to me, full speed, and leaped on me. His feet went off my chest, and he shot straight up and caught that ball!

"And he did it without spiking me. I still can't figure how I didn't get cut. He ran right up me and scared me to death. He made the damndest catch I've ever seen, and I still don't know how he did it. I couldn't believe it. I told him I didn't know if he was good, or just crazy."

The Giants' Genius

When Bill Rigney managed the Giants, he viewed Willie Mays as more or less a player-coach. Rig had a high regard for his superstar's baseball intelligence and often used Mays as a model of how to play the game.

"If you want to play for me, you'll have to learn one thing," Rigney would tell his new infielders. "If they hit the ball to the center fielder, you go to a base. Never mind whether you think he's going to throw it to you. Just be there. He knows things you never thought about."

"What things?" a young infielder once asked the manager.

"I don't know," Rig replied. "I haven't thought of them either. I'm just telling you one thing, and you'd better believe it— Willie knows."

Turns out that Mays truly did some managing while patrolling center field, positioning players and often calling the pitches. He explained:

"I managed the field," he said. "The other players played off me, like a quarterback. I would tap my head for a fastball, my chest for a breaking ball and my knee for a change-up. The catcher would give them to the pitcher.

"Herman Franks gave me that authority. Whatever went on, I did it. I did everything. I set the defenses, infield and outfield, and I called the pitches. We had one rule. If you didn't follow what I did, you didn't play."

Willie's Greatest Day

It was Sunday, April 30, 1961, and when Willie Mays awoke at the Giants' downtown hotel in Milwaukee, he was sick to his stomach after eating some barbequed ribs the previous night. When he arrived at County Stadium weak and weary, he told manager Alvin Dark, "I don't think I can make it."

During batting practice, infielder Joey Amalfitano walked up to Mays and suggested he use his bat. Mays walked into the batting cage with his teammate's lumber, and the balls started flying out of the ballpark.

"Every ball I hit, for the first six balls, goes out," Mays recalled, "and I said, 'Joey, something's wrong here.' So, I got to the lineup card, scratch a guy's name out—I don't know who it was—and put my name in."

On his first two at-bats, Mays homered off Braves starter Lew Burdette. Then he connected off Seth Morehead and Don McMahon for a total of four, and was in the on-deck circle when Jim Davenport made the last out of the ninth inning.

"Greatest day of my career," he said. "When I hit the two off Burdette, I think I'm through for the day because you don't uusually get but two. I made an out off Moe Drabowsky, a liner to [Hank] Aaron in center field. There were a lot of home runs hit that day."

In fact, there were 10 hit by both clubs, including two apiece by Aaron and Giants shortstop Jose Pagan. But it was Mays's day as he accumulated eight RBI and became the ninth player in history to hit four in one game. Since that memorable day, only four others have done it, including Mike Cameron and Shawn Green in 2002.

The Giants tied the major-league record with eight home runs, including solos by Felipe Alou and Orlando Cepeda. The previous day, they hit five out of the yard in a 7-3 victory, tying the National League record of 13 in two games. Two were hit by Willie McCovey, and one each by Felipe Alou, Jim Davenport and Cepeda.

What isn't commonly known is that McCovey was partly responsible for Mays's upset stomach. Dark, instituting a get-tough policy, took away single-room privileges and had the two Willies sharing a room in Milwaukee. It was McCovey who ordered the ribs.

Born to Play Himself

Early in his career, Willie Mays was asked to appear on a television show, and the director asked him how he planned to play himself.

A perplexed Mays quickly replied: "I don't know. Just turn those cameras on, and if it ain't me, let me know."

The Miracle Man

It took a while for Northern California fans to warm up to Willie Mays, and the final stages of the 1962 season certainly accelerated the process. On the final day, his eighth-inning homer produced a 2-1 victory over the Houston Colt .45s and enabled the Giants to tie the Dodgers, forcing a playoff.

Then, his two home runs and a single in Game 1 powered an 8-0 thumping of the Dodgers. Two days later, the Giants entered the ninth inning at Dodger Stadium trailing 4-2. Mays's single knocked in the first run, and he capped a four-run rally by scoring for a 6-4 victory and the pennant.

"With two runs down in the ninth, who would give a nickel for our chances?" a disbelieving Mays said amid the clubhouse din. "Honestly, I never thought we'd do it. This is my third World Series, and the other two were nothing like this one. But who cares about the Yankees? The important thing was beating the Dodgers."

A Good-Luck Charm

Prior to the decisive Game 3 of the 1962 playoff series with the Dodgers, a reporter approached Giants manager Alvin Dark and informed him that L.A. coach Leo Durocher, the manager of the pennant-winning 1951 Giants, remembered that miracle team.

"Durocher brought the same T-shirt he had worn in the 1951 playoff final—did you bring any memento of that game?" the reporter asked.

"Yeah," Dark replied, "Willie Mays."

Willie Wonders

In a controversial ending to the 1962 World Series, Matty Alou was on first base with two outs in the bottom of the ninth inning of Game 7 and Willie Mays doubled to right. The ball was slowed by the rain-soaked turf, Roger Maris made a quick retrieve, and third base coach Whitey Lockman held Alou at third.

Willie McCovey followed with a scorching liner to second baseman Bobby Richardson for the final out. The New York Yankees won the game 1-0, and the consensus was that Lockman acted wisely. Mays, however, was left wondering what might have happened if he had been at first base.

"I would have liked to have been the baserunner and had somebody else hit the double," Mays said many years later. "I would have tried to score somehow, and we would have had a good time at home plate. Either [catcher] Elston Howard would have hit me out, or I would have hit him. But you can't blame Matty. No one would ever want to make the last out."

Holding Court

Barry Bonds often speaks fondly of his youth in the Giants' clubhouse, where he idolized Willie Mays whenever he accompanied his father Bobby to Candlestick Park in 1968-74. But Mays held court for his teammates' sons long before that.

"He played with all our kids," recalled Jack Sanford, a 24-game winner on the 1962 National League champions. "They'd all pester us every day to take 'em out to the ballpark. They'd beg us to bring 'em out with us in the morning.

"Then, when they got there, they'd forget all about old dads. They'd all be sitting at Willie's locker every day, like it was a little classroom. The kids just always loved Willie and being around him."

What an Encore

On Sept. 13, 1965, at the Astrodome, Willie Mays became the fourth player in major-league history to hit 500 home runs. He did it with a 450-foot bolt to center off Don Nottebart, leading off the fourth inning and triggering a 5-1 victory over the Houston Astros. A crowd of 19,827 gave him a long standing ovation.

That milestone homer truly was significant, but it was surpassed on the thrill charts by what transpired under glass the next night. Entering the ninth inning, the Astros had a 5-2 lead when Bob Bruce walked Bob Burda with one out. Claude Raymond took over and Dick Schofield grounded out. Jesus Alou singled for 5-3, bringing Mays to the plate.

Mays, going for a game-tying home run, swung so hard at two Raymond fasrtballs that he fell to the ground. After the count reached 3-2, Raymond kept challenging him with fastballs, and he fouled off four more pitches. Then Raymond fired a 10th fastball to Mays, who deposited it over the left field wall for a 5-5 tie.

"That," Schofield said, "is like challenging God." And after Jim Davenport's 10th-inning single produced a 7-5 victory, the Giants' 12th in a row, Len Gabrielson declared in amazement: "Everyone in the stadium knew he was going for the home run, and he went and got it—greatest thing I ever saw."

Following his dramatic homer, his 48th of an MVP year, Mays summed up: "I kept waiting for a breaking ball, but all he threw me was fastballs. But it wasn't the homer that thrilled me—it was the way all those guys reacted. I'll never forget the way they carried on."

Curiously, among those who carried on was teammate Warren Spahn. The Hall of Fame lefty was with the Giants briefly that season, having the distinction of seeing No. 1 and No. 500 of Mays's career. That's because he gave up Willie's first major-league hit, a home run, in 1951.

Beating the Dodgers

Willie Mays always had some of his best success against the dreaded Dodgers, and the 1965 season was no exception. On the day of the infamous Marichal-Roseboro incident, Mays acted as a peacemaker until order was restored. Then he homered off Sandy Koufax to win that emotional game for the Giants.

When the season concluded, Mays beat Koufax again. Although the Dodgers edged the Giants for the pennant, Mays was voted the National League MVP with 224 points. Koufax finished second with 177, and Dodgers teammate Maury Wills was third with 164.

"Beating Koufax is a great thrill," Mays said after becoming San Francisco's first MVP. "It's just wonderful to be chosen with so many other good ballplayers around. But I'd rather have won the pennant than the award."

The 1965 season rivaled 1962 as Mays's greatest in S.F. He set a franchise record with 52 home runs, leading the majors, and also had a league-leading .645 slugging percentage with 112 RBIs and a .317 batting average.

Move Over, Mel

After Willie Mays hit his 511th home run to tie ex-Giant Mel Ott for the most in National League history, April 24, 1966, he couldn't wait to hit the next one. But he admittedly was feeling the pressure when he went into a three-for-21 slump while swinging for the fences.

The misery continued on May 4, when the Dodgers visited Candlestick Park and crafty lefty Claude Osteen struck him out on his first two at-bats. But on the first pitch Mays saw in the fifth inning, he hammered a high outside change-up and took it the other way, over the right field screen for No. 512.

"Sure, I've been pressing," Mays confessed afterward. "But now it's over and I can go back to just playing baseball. But there's Ted Williams [521] and Jimmie Foxx [534], and it'll be happening again, right?"

Mays was correct in his assessment, but for the time being, the pressure was off. After the record-breaking homer, a crowd of 28,220 gave him the longest and loudest standing ovation in Candlestick Park's brief baseball history, and he answered the "We want Willie!" chants by emerging from the dugout and tipping his cap.

"It was a milestone to Willie's career, but just another lousy home run to me," Osteen said after the Giants' 5-1 victory. In fact, it was Mays' 85th "lousy" homer off Dodgers pitching (more than any other team), including 41 off Brooklyn pitchers.

A Sense of Relief

There was jubilation when Willie Mays homered to right at Candlestick Park off Ray Washburn of the St. Louis Cardinals,

Aug. 17, 1966, to pass Jimmie Foxx and become the No. 2 home run hitter of all time. But No. 535 left Mays more relieved than excited because the pursuit of home run milestones left him mentally drained.

"I'm sure glad all this is over," Mays said following the Giants' 4-3 victory. "Now I've passed all the guys I'm going to, and maybe everyone will leave me alone. I sure hope so, anyway. It's been a long season already, and I think it's been a little unfair to the rest of the guys."

Of course, he was asked about reaching Babe Ruth's 714 home runs, to which Mays realistically replied: "Man, that's an awful lot of homers. And when you figure I'm 35 now, you almost have to bet I don't have a chance to catch him. I don't think I can do it."

If Mays wasn't overwhelmed by his fourth-inning shot off Washburn, plate umpire Chris Pelekoudas certainly was. When Mays reached the plate following his 380-foot shot, the veteran ump extended his hand and grabbed Willie's.

"We're supposed to be impartial, and I suppose an umpire shouldn't do a thing like that, but when a man reaches baseball immortality..." explained Pelekoudas, who later apologized to National League president Warren Giles.

"I didn't know what I was doing," Pelekoudas said.

"Yes, you did," a forgiving Giles replied.

Calling His Shot

When godson Barry Bonds hit his 600th home run in 2002, it was a major event before a sellout crowd at Pacific Bell Park. When Willie Mays did it, Sept. 22, 1969, there were 4,779 in the stands in San Diego, and he wasn't even in the Giants' lineup.

But Mays that night did something unique. As the game with the Padres reached the late innings, the message board told the fans: "Come tomorrow night and see Willie hit No. 600."

According to teammates, when Mays looked at the scoreboard he quipped: "Tomorrow night? I'm going to hit it tonight."

So in the top of the seventh of a 2-2 tie, manager Clyde King summoned Mays to bat for rookie George Foster with a man on and no outs. He promptly delievered as promised, sending right-hander Mike Corkins's first-pitch fastball nearly 400 feet to left-center.

"Not many guys will come close to hitting 600, so I'm really thrilled," a weary Mays said following the 4-2 victory. "Maybe Hank Aaron will do it. I've been trying to hit home runs lately, and maybe trying too hard.

"I don't know how much longer I can go, but I know I'll hit some more home runs if I stay healthy. That's been my trouble. I've been out of the lineup and it's been tough getting my timing back."

The Awards Flow

Willie Mays's 1969 season wasn't among his best (13 homers, 58 RBI), but it was rewarding. In addition to home run No. 600, he soon was named Player of the Decade by *The Sporting News* and the No. 1 All-Time Giant in a fans' poll conducted in conjunction with baseball's centennial festivities.

It was a decade dominated by great pitching, yet Mays averaged 35 home runs a season, including a career-high 52 as the National League MVP in 1965 and 49 when he powered the Giants to the pennant in 1962. He averaged 100.3 RBIs and 105.1 runs during the decade.

On the mythical Giants All-Star squad, third baseman Jim Davenport was the only other San Francisco player to make the franchise team. The S.F. All-Stars were Willie McCovey, 1B; Ron Hunt, 2B; Hal Lanier, SS; Harvey Kuenn, LF; Felipe Alou, RF; Tom Haller, C; Juan Marichal, RHP; Johnny Antonelli, LHP; Davenport, and Mays.

Mays vs. Aaron

Several former players from the 1960s contend that if Henry Aaron played his home games at Candlestick Park and Willie

Mays had the benefit of home games in Milwaukee and Atlanta, the Giants' superstar would have finished with more home runs than all-time leader Aaron, who finished with 755—and few in San Francisco.

"I think Candlestick hurt everybody," said Mays, who hit 660 home runs. "We'd only hit about one dozen homers to left all season before the ballpark was enclosed (1972). I knew it was going to be tough when I took BP before the first game there. I couldn't hit a ball over the fence in left.

"I started going to an inside-out swing and hitting more to right. But we didn't complain. Nobody wanted to play there, so it gave us an edge. We just didn't think negatively."

Mr. July

What Reggie Jackson was to October, Willie Mays was to July, the month the All-Star Game is played. Mays was the Nationals' finest All-Star performer, winning games with his bat, his glove and his speed while compiling a .307 average in 24 appearances, including .417 in his first 14 games.

"The American League was the enemy, and I tried to play as hard as I could," Mays said. "I felt we were the better league, so I really wanted to do well in those games. My [All-Star] records don't mean anything. The main thing was winning.

"It was just like a family. We were all extremely proud to play in that game, and winning it was extremely important. We had sort of an unwritten rule that guys like myself, Clemente and Aaron would play the full nine innings."

Mays's All-Star highlights were numerous, and they were especially meaningful after the team moved to California. In 1959, at Forbes Field, his walkoff triple in the bottom of the ninth produced a 5-4 victory.

Nobody enjoyed a better year in All-Star history than Mays during a two-game NL sweep at Kansas City and Yankee Stadium. He had six hits in eight at-bats, including a double, a triple and a home run to pace 5-4 and 6-0 victories.

The two-time All-Star MVP regards the 1963 game at Cleveland as his finest. He stole two bases, scored twice, had a pair of RBI and deprived Joe Pepitone of extra bases with a fine catch in a 5-3 victory.

I Didn't Want to Go

One of Willie Mays's toughest days with the Giants was his last. It was May 11, 1972, and financially strapped owner Horace Stoneham did the unthinkable, trading perhaps the greatest Giant of them all to the New York Mets for nondescript pitcher Charlie Williams. Even though Stoneham did it for Mays's security, it still was difficult.

"I really didn't want to go," he recalled. "I had a feeling the trade was coming up, and if I had made enough money, I wouldn't have gone. I would have just said, 'Say hey, I quit.' But I loved baseball too much. I wanted to play as long as I could.

"What really helped me was [Mets owner] Mrs. Joan Payson. I was ready to go home, and she called me in Montreal. I had my bags packed. She called and said, 'I always wanted you to be a Met. I want you to be back in New York. Write your own contract, and whatever you want, you've got it.' I went back and played one more year."

When he retired following the 1973 World Series (he batted .286 against the A's), Mays's career numbers included a .302 batting average, 2,992 games, 3,283 hits, 2,062 runs, 1,903 RBI and, of course, the 660 home runs.

In 1979, the year he was inducted into the Hall of Fame, Mays was asked who was the greatest player he ever saw?

"I thought I was," Mays said, and many would agree.

What They'd Say About Hey

"Willie Mays is the only player who can help a team simply by riding on the bus with it."
—*Charley Grimm*

"With a uniform on, there was no one smarter. He was alert, quick as a cat and never missed a sign. I'd rate him with Eddie Stanky, Alvin Dark and Pee Wee Reese as the smartest players I managed."

—*Leo Durocher*

"The greatest all-around player in the history of baseball. He's the only man I know who can win a game for you in every department of the game, except pitching."

—*Bill Rigney*

"Willie's power is essentially to left center, so he had to make himself all over when he left the Polo Grounds. To get the ball up in the wind at Candlestick, he had to go the other way. The mark of a great hitter is his ability to adjust. Mays did it."

—*Stan Musial*

"He is the greatest player of all time. If I had to have one man to do the job on a play or a time at bat that is going to win or lose a pennant, I would pick Willie Mays."

—*Hank Aaron*

Willie McCovey:
The Most Popular Giant

Club Made Accurate Assessment
in Keeping Original Big Mac

A Dazzling Debut

It would be difficult to imagine a more impressive major-league debut than the one Willie McCovey enjoyed on July 30, 1959. He walloped two triples and two singles, scoring three runs and driving in two during a 7-2 victory over fellow future Hall of Famer Robin Roberts of the Philadelphia Phillies at Seals Stadium.

What made it even more astounding was that McCovey was thrust into the starting lineup following a sleepless night in Phoenix and an early-morning flight to San Francisco.

"I didn't even find out I got called up until after a double-header in Phoenix, so I was up all night packing," he explained. "The next morning, I took an early flight, was met at the airport, rushed to the ballpark and right away, I'm in the starting lineup.

"It all happened so fast, and before I knew it, I was in the ballgame hitting third and banging out hits all over Seals Stadium. If I would have had time to think about it, I probably would have been nervous and probably wouldn't have broken in the way I did."

Added manager Bill Rigney after McCovey became the first player with four hits in his major-league debut since Casey Stengel in 1912: "In batting practice, he hit a couple of balls where you knew from the sound of the bat this was going to be something special. That day, he was awesome."

*Willie McCovey earned MVP honors in 1969, hitting .320, with 45
home runs and 126 RBI. McCovey quickly became the most feared
hitter in the National League. (AP/WWP)*

And That's Not All

McCovey's sensational debut is storybook stuff, but he was a lot more in 1959 than a one-day wonder. One day later, his eighth-inning single scored Willie Mays with the winning run against Pittsburgh. He followed with two doubles and a single against the Pirates in his third game and hit his first homer in his fourth game.

"The Giants won six of the first seven games McCovey played in, during which time he collected five singles, two doubles, two triples and three home runs," announcer Russ Hodges recalled. "He was the talk of baseball."

McCovey's infusion kept the Giants in contention until the final week. He batted .354 with 13 home runs in roughly one-third of a season and had a 22-game hitting streak. The short stint was so impressive, he unanimously was named National League Rookie of the Year over candidates like Maury Wills and George Altman.

Manager Bill Rigney, a little carried away, declared: "With the wind blowing out to right at Candlestick Park, there's no telling what a lefty swinger of McCovey's talents might hit. His hands travel with lightning speed. He packs the power of a good fighter's right-handed punch. What a picture swing. He could even be baseball's next .400 hitter."

A Full-time Left Fielder

Despite the ongoing controversry of whether McCovey or Orlando Cepeda should be the first baseman during their early years with the Giants, McCovey never saw it as a conflict. In fact, once he was switched to left field by manager Alvin Dark in 1961, he wanted to stay there.

"I knew the Giants would be better off with both of us in the lineup," Mac reasoned. "I figured they were going to find a spot for both of us. I played first until Alvin switched us around, and when I went to left field, I felt I was out there to stay.

"I had no intention of ever coming back to first base. As a matter of fact, I really didn't want to come back because when the switch was made, it worked out so well. We went to the World Series [1962], and I led the league in home runs [1963] and made the All-Star team as a left fielder.

"I thought I was going to spend the rest of my career out there. I figured we'd both stay with the Giants for the next 15 or 20 years at those two positions. But then Cepeda got hurt and I was forced to come back and play first because he was out the whole [1964] season.

"I never regretted going to left field one bit. You really don't have to think that much to play outfield. You can stand out there and concentrate on your hitting a lot. And with Willie Mays playing center, you weren't going to get burned too much."

Words of Wisdom

There's no question McCovey was the most feared left-handed hitter of his era, as New York Mets manager Casey Stengel strongly suggested when he and pitcher Roger Craig, the future Giants manager, were discussing some pregame strategy on facing Big Mac.

"Mr. Craig," Stengel inquired, "where would you like me to position the right fielder—in the upper deck or the lower deck?"

Destroying Dandy Don

When Willie McCovey retired, he thanked Don Drysdale for "hitting my bat so often," and that definitely wasn't a stretch. Among McCovey's 521 career home runs, 12 were struck off the Dodgers' fearless right-hander, including six game winners.

In fact, when McCovey struggled to establish himself as a Giants regular in 1959-62, Drysdale was his confidence builder. In a two-year-plus period between April 30, 1960, and July 11, 1962, Stretch hit seven home runs against the Dodgers—all off Dandy Don.

"You couldn't find a more perfect match of a hitter's swing and a pitcher's delivery—it was brutal," said Dodgers closer Ron Perranoski, who observed the carnage. "Nobody said anything to Don because of the competitor he was."

Nobody had to. Through 1963, McCovey had 10 home runs and a .444 average against Drysdale before the Dodger became more cautious than challenging. Still, he was Stretch's favorite target. Don Sutton, Larry Jackson and Phil Niekro were far back, each yielding eight homers to McCovey.

"He gave me as much trouble as anybody ever did," Drysdale acknowledged. "Those first few years, he just beat on me like a tom-tom, and I was bullheaded enough to keep trying to pitch to him. He wasn't hitting 1.000, so somebody had to be getting him out—and it sure wasn't me."

Although he was a platoon player at the time, Giants managers made sure McCovey had his whacks at Drysdale, off whom Stretch was 19 for 35 with seven homers at one stage. That prompted Jim Murray to write: "He doesn't hit batting practice pitchers that well. If it were a bullfight, he'd get Don's ears."

After Drysdale retired to the broadcast booth, he was announcing a spring training game in Palm Springs when McCovey connected off Nolan Ryan. Giants announcer Lon Simmons rushed over to Drysdale and said: "You can't even get him out when you're announcing."

A Rare Double

By 1969, McCovey was the most feared batter in the NL, and he showed it on all stages. His 45 homers, 126 RBI and .320 average were the highlights of a career year crowned with MVP honors. A bonus was earning the MVP trophy at the All-Star Game, played at RFK Stadium in Washington D.C.

The Nationals were ahead 3-1 when Hank Aaron opened the third with a single and McCovey followed with a two-run homer off Blue Moon Odom. One inning later, his solo homer off Denny McLain enabled Big Mac to join Arky Vaughn, Ted

Williams and Al Rosen as the only two-homer All-Stars at the time.

"It's exciting and a big thrill to play in these games," McCovey allowed following the 9-3 NL romp, its seventh consecutive victory. "I like to hit home runs any time, but they still don't count in the statistics."

The sensational season made McCovey the first man in NL history to win league home run, RBI and slugging (.656) titles two years in a row. American Leaguers Babe Ruth and Jimmie Foxx were the only others to do it. He also became only the second NL slugger with back-to-back homer-RBI crowns, joining Bill Nicholson of the Cubs.

In the MVP race, Stretch and Mets ace Tom Seaver each received 11 first-place votes (out of 24), but McCovey had more seconds and outpointed Seaver 265-243. Hank Aaron was third with 188.

Going, Going, Gone

Some of Willie McCovey's tape-measure home runs attained legendary stature, and the original Big Mac (before Mark McGwire) hit perhaps his longest at Busch Stadium off Al Jackson, sending a ball screaming far into the upper deck.

"Despite all the bombs McGwire was hitting there, I got a call from Jack Buck in 1998, and he said mine was still the longest hit there," McCovey said. "That made me feel good."

McCovey also became the only player to belt a baseball over the deck beyond the right field fence at Cincinnati's Crosley Field. And in the few years the Montreal Expos used Jarry Park, a city playground, for their home games, he would splash homers into the community pool.

He also recalled Forbes Field in Pittsburgh, where center field was so deep that the Pirates stored their batting cage there during games. Steve Blass was pitching, and McCovey cleared the cage, recalling: "They figured nobody could hit it that far."

A Rare Double Double

As part of his inspiring comeback in 1977, McCovey became the first man in history to hit two home runs in one inning—twice. During a 10-run sixth inning at Cincinnati, June 27, Stretch entered the record books with his slugging spree in a 14-9 romp.

McCovey hit a solo homer off Jack Billingham, and later that same inning connected for a grand slam off Joe Hoerner. On April 12, 1973, against the Houston Astros, he homered off Ken Forsch and Jim Crawford in an eight-run fourth inning during a 9-3 rout.

On that day, Stretch joined a list of eight National Leaguers to twice homer in one inning and became the first Giant to do it since Sid Gordon in 1949. Andre Dawson later joined McCovey as the only sluggers to do it on two occasions.

"The whole thing is funny," McCovey said after his 1977 feat. "The day before, I was sitting in the dugout, and I was thinking of a list of all my home runs. I saw that I had hit two in one inning, and I wondered if I would ever do that again. I did it the next night."

Isn't It Just Grand?

When Willie McCovey connected twice that 1977 night in Cincinnati, he entered the record books in more ways than one. The grand slam that inning was the 17th of his career, breaking a tie with Hank Aaron for the most in National League history. He's still No. 1 in the NL and second all-time behind Lou Gehrig, who had 23 "salamis."

"Of course I was aware of it, and I'm happy I got it," McCovey said of No. 17. "But I've always been such an admirer of Hank Aaron because we're both from the same hometown [Mobile, Ala.] and we played sandlot ball together. I would have been content to retire with a tie."

Curiously, 11 of his 17 slams were hit at Candlestick Park, including one against the Giants' Tom Bradley in 1974 as a member of the San Diego Padres. He hit 15 in a San Francisco uniform, beginning with No. 1 against Carlton Willey of the Mikwaukee Braves, June 12, 1960, at The Stick.

Cincinnati was the team he victimized most, hitting four grand slams against the Reds. Three of the 17 were as a pinch hitter, tying the record held by Ron Northey and Rich Reese. He hit one off a Hall of Famer—Don Sutton on July 2, 1972—and had a pair off New York Mets relief ace Tug McGraw, Sept. 27, 1967, and May 10, 1970.

A Humbled Hero

McCovey was way past his prime when he rejoined the Giants in 1977 and enjoyed a second wind as the NL Comeback Player of the Year. The fans appreciated his return, and 24,426 showed up Sept. 18 for Willie McCovey Day at Candlestick Park.

The Cincinnati Reds had a 2-0 lead entering the bottom of the eighth, but the Giants rallied for a tie with two runs, setting the stage for a storybook finish in the ninth. McCovey's single off Pedro Borbon produced a 3-2 victory.

"Without a doubt, this is one of the great moments of my career," he said. "So much happened to me that year that kind of overshadowed all the things I'd done when I was really having the super years, and that hit stood out.

"I'd never been given a 'day' before, and to drive in the winning run on your day, after they've given you all those gifts and you know that 90 percent of the people in the stands are there to see you—that's special."

What made it more special was that Willie's mother was in attendance, watching him play a major-league game for only the second time. A rejuvenated McCovey played 141 games that season, his most since 1969, and finished with a .280 average, 28 homers and 86 RBI.

Bittersweet Blast

Willie McCovey joined the exclusive 500 Home Run Club, June 30, 1978, in Atlanta, yet it wasn't a totally joyous occasion. Only 14,429 were present at Fulton County Stadium, and the Braves clobbered the Giants 10-6, 10-9 on a steamy night in Georgia.

McCovey, age 40 at the time, connected off Jamie Easterly in the second inning of the opener, an off-field shot to left that created a 1-1 tie. He circled the bases and received a standing ovation. Pitcher John Curtis retrieved the ball and accompanied the rest of the bullpen on a dash to greet Willie Mac at home plate.

"Naturally, a little edge on the thrill was lost when we were swept, because winning the pennant is our priority, not my personal goals," said McCovey, whose Giants held a three-game division lead following the double defeat.

"But I'm glad it's over. In spring training, I'd thought I'd get the 500 by the end of April. I wanted to hit it at home, but when I hadn't during the last homestand, I forgot about that. I was going to two good ballparks for me, San Diego and Atlanta, and I figured I might get it done in one of them."

Curiously, on the same night, fellow first baseman Mike Ivie, who eventually was given McCovey's job, hit his record second pinch-hit grand slam of the season in the first game. And also of historical significance that day, Larry Doby was named manager of the Chicago White Sox, 30 years after becoming the first American Leaguer to break the color barrier.

The Last One

It was May 3, 1980, relatively early in the season, when Willie McCovey took Montreal Expos pitcher Scott Sanderson deep at Olympic Stadium. It was his first home run since Aug. 25, and No. 521 of his career. Nobody realized it would be his last.

"He'll get a lot more," manager Dave Bristol said. "He thinks he can play forever, and what's wrong with thinking that way? Maybe he will. He's in great shape."

There wasn't much commotion over the home run, but backup catcher Mike Sadek chased it down beyond the right field fence, inscribed "No. 521" on the ball and added it to his memorabilia collection.

"I turned on a fastball, and he's got a good one," McCovey said of the home run, also unaware of its significance at the time. "Sure, it felt good. I can't remember any of the 521 that weren't satisfying."

As it turned out, it was a truly memorable home run. It tied him with Ted Williams on the all-time list, making them the most prolific left-handed home run hitters behind Babe Ruth. That year, he also joined boyhood idol Williams among baseball's few four-decade players and finished with 469 home runs as a Giant, the most in S.F. history.

Rising to the Occasion

As he did in 1977, McCovey maintained his sense of drama during his farewell tour in 1980. Joining an elite group of four-decade players, Stretch had a rough final year, but there were highlights.

Retiring at midseason, McCovey played his final game at Dodger Stadium, July 10. He batted as a pinch hitter and hit a sacrifice fly off Rick Sutcliffe in the eighth inning for a 4-3 lead in an eventual extra-inning victory. In a touching tribute, the capacity crowd of 46,244 gave him a long standing ovation.

"One of the greatest moments of my baseball career," summed up McCovey, who was feted throughout the National League that season while being coaxed into retirement to make room for Mike Ivie and rookie Rich Murray, Eddie's brother.

Giants coach Jim Lefebvre, a former Dodger, added: "That's the first time I've ever seen an opposing player get an ovation like that here. Baseball's going to miss him. He's one of the last guys who really electrified people, who had that special charisma. He couldn't have gone out in better style. The great ones always rise to the occasion."

Summed up McCovey, who played until age 42 despite gimpy knees: "I never let things set me back. Unfortunately, I didn't have the smoothest career, but I always considered myself to be a good athlete. I always wanted to be up in the key situations.

"I was fortunate to be able to play that long, and I attribute it to exercise and diet. They contributed to my last five years being relatively injury-free, so my so-called comeback didn't surprise me.

"I never thought I was gone."

What They'd Say About Stretch

"He's the strongest man in baseball. Guys like Frank Howard and Harmon Killebrew can hit them far, but they're pull hitters. Stretch can hit them deep to any part of the ballpark."
—*Willie Mays*

"Early in my career, I was convinced the Giants' manager manipulated the lineup so McCovey would always come to bat in the ninth inning. Every time the game was on the line, I had to look at McCovey. They had guys like Mays and Hart, but it always came down to McCovey. He was awesome, easily the most feared hitter in the league."
—*Don Sutton*

"Being back in San Francisco must have something to do with it, because the fans respond to him and he's playing with enthusiasm. You can see that he takes good care of himself. I've never heard anyone say a bad word about him."
—*Pete Rose in 1977*

"You don't appreciate a guy like that until you have a chance to play on the same club. He just gets the job done, day in and day out. He's been our whole team, our leader, our MVP."
—*Bill Madlock*

"I was a kid at Seals Stadium the day he made his debut and got four hits off Robin Roberts, and not one of those balls was hit soft."

—*Joe Morgan*

"He made a big impression on me when I was coming up with the Giants. He didn't say much, but he set an example by what he did. I just watched and learned."

—*George Foster*

"I hated to pitch to him outside because I was always afraid he'd hit one back through the box. You could pitch him up and in, but you'd better put it right where you wanted it. He made you pay for a mistake."

—*Roger Craig*

"He used to scare me the most when I was playing first base. I was just praying he wouldn't hit one down the line. He was so strong, one of the most awesome players I've ever seen."

—*Joe Torre*

"The great ones are better for a reason, more than their physical skills. They've got something that's beyond the rest of us. Mac's the type of guy you can't forget. I'm sad and happy at the same time. I'm glad he went out the way he did, but I wish he could go on playing forever."

—*Darrell Evans on McCovey's final game*

"Like our cable cars, Willie McCovey will endure in the hearts of all of those who love San Francisco."

—*S.F. Mayor Dianne Feinstein*

Juan Marichal: Unhittable And Unappreciated

Dominican Dandy Won Games, Not Awards in Remarkable Career

An Immediate Hit

Unlike Sandy Koufax, to whom he was compared for pitching excellence in the 1960s, Juan Marichal was not a slow bloomer. At 19, the high-kicking rookie from the Dominican Republic was dazzling minor league hitters.

After going 21-8 with a 1.87 ERA and 246 strikeouts his first year (1958) at Michigan City, Marichal was 18-13 with a 2.39 ERA as a second-year pro at Springfield, Mass. In those two years, he incredibly completed 47 of 60 starts.

When he got off to a 7-1 start with a 2.01 ERA at Triple-A Tacoma in 1960, it seemed certain the major leagues weren't far away. When he reached the Giants to stay that summer, The Dominican Dandy had completed 59 of 78 minor league starts, striking out 575 batters while walking merely 131 in 655 innings.

"He can throw all of his pitches overhand, three-quarters and sidearm," enthused Tacoma manager Red Davis. "And what's best of all is his control of all those pitches and his confidence. He can use anything in his repertoire with full assurance that he's going to get it over the plate."

The Lifesaver

To hear Juan Marichal tell it, he may never have enjoyed a Hall of Fame career were it not for Felipe Alou, his friend, teammate and Dominican Republic skin diving partner. It was during a day in the Caribbean waters that Alou made sure his buddy would live to pitch another day.

"He saved me because I obeyed one of the four rules of skin diving, but violated another," Marichal explained. "I violated the one that has to do with knowing your limitations.

"I swam too much, too hard and too fast. I got cramps and I knew I was sinking. But I obeyed the rule that says you never dive alone. Felipe was with me, so he saved me."

Alou insists the story is true, adding: "Juan was fearless in the water, but he also was a little foolish. He wasn't afraid of anything, but I was a little more careful and I watched out for him."

Getting His Kicks

The high leg kick that became a Marichal trademark was learned by necessity when the young sidearm pitcher reported to Class-A Springfield (Mass.) for the 1959 season and came under the tutelage of manager Andy Gilbert.

"He told me I was too young to throw sidearm," Marichal recalled, "so I started throwing overhand and the pitches started coming in high. Andy told me to kick higher with my leg.

"He explained that a high kick would bring the ball down because the body force would be coming down when I released the ball. I had a good season [18-13, 2.39 ERA, 23 complete games and 208 strikeouts] and was in the big-league camp the next year."

Almost Perfect

The San Francisco Hall of Famers made sensational major-league debuts, and Juan Marichal was no exception. It was July 19, 1960, at Candlestick Park, and the young right-hander was starting a night game against the Philadelphia Phillies.

Tony Taylor and Bobby DelGreco, the first two Phillies, struck out and a legendary career was born. Orlando Cepeda's double and Jim Davenport's single staked Marichal to a 1-0 lead in the second inning and the rookie retired the first 19 Phillies.

An error by shortstop Eddie Bressoud snapped the streak, but Marichal entered the eighth inning with a no-hitter. With two outs, pinch hitter Clay Dalrymple lined a low curve sharply to center for the Phillies' lone hit.

"Everyone commented about the high kick and the ungainly physical posture this delivery produced after the ball was released," Marichal told biographer Charles Einstein. "I would have to agree. I do not think I will ever be classified as one of the greatest fielding pitchers."

The First No-Hitter

No Giant had ever pitched a no-hitter since Carl Hubbell in 1929, but Juan Marichal didn't have to wait long to show he had the stuff to do it. Three years following his one-hit debut in 1960, Marichal held the Houston Colt .45s hitless, June 15, 1963, before 18,869 at Candlestick Park.

"You never think about no-hitters," Marichal recalled following his retirement. "Even in the seventh inning that day, I wasn't thinking about a no-hitter because I didn't think I had my best stuff that day.

"But when I came out for the last two innings, I had the greatest stuff I ever had in my life. I struck out a few batters, and Willie McCovey saved the no-hitter in left field. Carl Warwick almost hit a ball out, but Mac was so tall, he reached up and grabbed it."

Marichal had to be at his best because Houston's Dick Drott was nearly as effective, matching Juan's shutout through seven innings. Doubles by Jim Davenport and Chuck Hiller in the eighth produced a 1-0 victory.

But not before Marichal worked a one-two-three ninth. Johnny Temple batted for Drott and hit a foul pop to Orlando Cepeda at first base. Pinch hitter Pete Runnels struck out. Then Brock Davis was called out on strikes by umpire Ed Sudol on a 2-2 fastball, and history was made.

"His was better than mine," Hubbell said following the 89-pitch gem. "In mine, we scored early and often and beat the Pirates 11-0. Juan couldn't really go all-out until the ninth, because up till then the score had been 0-0."

Spahnie Made Me Do It

During his historic duel with Milwaukee Braves ace Warren Spahn, July 2, 1963, Marichal was asked by manager Alvin Dark if he was tiring as the game reached extra innings at Candlestick Park.

"I can't come out—a 42-year-old man is still pitching and I'm only 23," reasoned Marichal, referring to the seemingly ageless Spahn. The two men each worked into the 16th inning, when Willie Mays's homer gave the weary Marichal a 1-0 victory.

As was the case in his no-hitter, there was a link with Hubbell, then the Giants' farm director. The marathon came exactly 30 years after King Carl went 18 innings to defeat the St. Louis Cardinals 1-0 in 1933.

"My back is very sore, but tonight is beautiful," Marichal said after the brisk-paced game required merely 4:10. "It reminds me of one I pitched in Springfield [Mass.] in 1959. That night, I go 17 innings, and I lose 1-0."

Manager Alvin Dark, in total amzement, added: "Juan never appeared to be laboring. He didn't throw many breaking pitches, thus tiring his arm, but just kept slipping across the fastball with a loose and fluid motion. He got stronger."

All-Star of All-Stars

An argument could be made that Marichal was the greatest All-Star Game pitcher in history, a distinction that added to his reputation as sort of a consolation following a brilliant career that resulted in few trophies or pennants.

Imagine a dream team of American League All-Stars being limited to seven hits and one earned run over 18 innings by one pitcher, the equivalent of two complete games. Well, that's exactly what Marichal did in eight All-Star Games from 1962 to 1971.

Nobody did it better than Marichal during an era when the National League prided itself on its All-Star Game mastery. The Dominican Dandy took it seriously enough to fashion a 2-0 record and a 0.50 ERA against the AL elite, yielding one earned run in 18 innings.

"The All-Star Game was very important to me, so I always tried to do my best and win," said Marichal, who finished his All-Star career with 14 scoreless innings. "There was always talk about one league being better than the other.

"It just happened that I had my best stuff and was healthy when I pitched in the All-Star Game. I felt in complete control, and I take pride in that. Pitching in the All-Star Game was a big thrill for me. It was an honor to be selected."

Pitcher Of the Sixties

Marichal won 104 more games than any pitcher in San Francisco history—238 to Gaylord Perry's 134—but most of the awards during his career went to Bob Gibson and Sandy Koufax, whose talent was embellished by postseason success.

But nobody was more effective during the pitching-rich sixties than The Dominican Dandy. During the decade, Marichal notched 191 victories and six 20-win seasons. Gibson won 164 games, reaching 20 on four occasions. Koufax had 137 victories in the sixties before retiring in 1966.

"Marichal was the finest pitcher I ever faced," Pittsburgh Pirates slugger Willie Stargell said. "I probably had more success against him than I did against Koufax, but I was in awe of Juan.

"I was in constant amazement of how he could get so many pitches over the plate. I remember a game when I struck out four times against Juan, all on different pitches—and he never threw the same pitch the same way twice."

Fellow Hall of Famer Frank Robinson concurred, adding: "Everyone marvelled at that high kick, much like Warren Spahn's. He was a natural in every sense. A lot of guys, Koufax for one, take years to put it together.

"But Juan was outstanding from the start. I had fair success with him, but you never felt comfortable at the plate because you couldn't anticipate what he was going to throw. He was a pain. There wasn't anyone better."

The Final Day

Marichal was on schedule to pitch the playoff opener with the Pittsburgh Pirates in 1971, but 16 losses in 23 games placed the Giants in a position to need a victory on the final day in San Diego to clinch despite leading the NL West since April 12.

It was Sept. 30, and Marichal rose to the occasion with a dazzling 81-pitch five-hitter that subdued the Padres 5-1. The Dominican Dandy finished with a flurry for a final 18-11 record, a good omen because it matched his record in pennant-winning 1962.

"They kept saying we were a dead horse, but who's dead now—they are," crowed Marichal, referring to the hated Dodgers and Billy Grabarkewitz, who had said: "We got a dead horse in front of us and we can't catch them."

The fact the Giants were 53-58 over the final four months didn't inspire confidence, and not having Marichal for two playoff starts gave the Pirates an edge that they exercised by winning three out of four and then stunning the Baltimore Orioles in the World Series.

"I remember Juan telling [manager] Charlie Fox before that final game that he could go ahead and order playoff tickets," Steve Stone recalled. "He beat San Diego and got us into the playoffs. We needed it, too, because the Dodgers also won."

What They'd Say About Juan

"Marichal had about six pitches, and he could throw them at any time and get them over. He could throw a screwball, a straight change, curve, fastball or slider at any given time and get it over. He could have been the best of all the right-handers in that time."

—Maury Wills

"You couldn't anticipate him. Juan had no set pattern. He had all that stuff, and he'd throw any of it in any situation. He was outstanding from the start, a natural in every sense of the word."

—*Frank Robinson*

"Koufax has two pitches, a fastball and a curve, and they're the two best pitches in the league. But Marichal has more. He has four or five, and he can control them all."

—*Mike Shannon*

"I remember the great battles Juan had with Roberto Clemente. They each had intense pride, so it was like the Dominican Republic against Puerto Rico. Juan was the finest pitcher I ever faced, definitely one of a kind."

—*Willie Stargell*

"Juan had the best control and the best command of any of the guys in the Sixties. A lot of guys threw harder and were better on specific pitches, but nobody had it all together like Juan."

—*Ferguson Jenkins*

"With Juan, the hitters never got the pitch they wanted. You had to hit *his* pitch. He was truly unique in that he had all the pitches, and I mean *all*. We didn't win any pennants those days, but it sure as heck wasn't Juan's fault."

—*Herman Franks*

"That foot is up in your face, and then he comes through like a charging fullback. He lunges right off the hill, and with all that confusion of motions, it's a problem seeing the ball. But his control is his biggest thing. He can throw all day within a two-inch space—in, out, up or down. I've never seen anyone as good as that."

—*Hank Aaron*

"The thing I hate about him is that it all looks so easy. With guys like Koufax and Drysdale, you can at least look out there and see the cords standing out on their neck. They look like they're working, like they're worried. Marichal just stands there, laughing at you."

—Gus Triandos

"If we made contact against Marichal, we considered it a hit. He had the control of Greg Maddux."

—Pat Corrales

Orlando Cepeda:
First Giants Hero

Baby Bull Won Hearts of Fans with Power

Better Late Than Never

It took more than 40 years, but Whitey Lockman made a prophetic assessment when he first watched Orlando Cepeda play baseball in spring training of 1958. Lockman was battling for the first base job with Bill White and the Puerto Rican rookie who was to become known as "The Baby Bull."

Manager Bill Rigney asked the veteran Lockman to take Cepeda under his wing and give him some insights on playing first base. Lockman was immediately impressed, and even more so when he saw the ball flying off Orlando's bat.

"How does he look, Whitey?" Rigney asked.

"This kid is a year away," Lockman replied.

"A year away from what?" Rigney inquired.

"From the Hall of Fame," Lockman declared.

Lockman explained his lofty appraisal: "I could tell early in spring training that Cepeda was the real deal. No question about it. There was no question about the way he swung the bat, and he was no donkey at first base. He was enthusiastic and strong."

A Dream Come True

One of the happiest days in Orlando Cepeda's baseball life was April 15, 1958, when the Giants played their first game in San Francisco and he was in the starting lineup against the Los Angeles Dodgers at Seals Stadium.

"I was very nervous," Cepeda recalled. "When I went out on the field, I started seeing all those big names like Gil Hodges,

Orlando Cepeda (AP/WWP)

Carl Furillo, Duke Snider and Don Newcombe. I was very impressed with those guys because I followed them so close.

"But when I was a kid, I was a New York Giants fan because of Ruben Gomez. He was a big hero in Puerto Rico, and here was Ruben pitching that game. It was a big day for everybody. Ruben pitched and Valmy Thomas caught, so we could communicate [in Spanish] pretty well."

It was a particularly great day for Cepeda, who immediately became a fan favorite by homering to right center off reliever Don Bessent in Gomez's six-hit, 8-0 victory before 23,448 in the historic West Coast opener.

Cepeda thereby became the first San Francisco Giants star to homer in his first game with the club, later being joined on an illustrious list by Bobby Bonds (1968), Darrell Evans (1976), Will Clark (1986), Kevin Mitchell (1987) and Barry Bonds (1993).

An Immediate Hit

Although Willie Kirkland was regarded as the rookie phenom when Giants camp opened in 1958, Cepeda's robust slugging soon grabbed the headlines. Correspondent Joe King, who covered the club in New York, was so impressed with Cepeda that he wired *The Sporting News* and extolled his virtues. The "Baseball Bible" named Cepeda its preseason Rookie of the Year—before he landed on the major-league roster.

Cepeda, of course, justified that by batting .312 with 25 homers and 96 RBI, thereby earning the real rookie honor. It didn't take long for the word to spread around the league that "The Baby Bull" was something special.

"I never form an opinion the first time around," Milwaukee Braves manager Fred Haney said in 1958. "The first time, we watch what a newcomer hits. The second time, we note what he *doesn't* hit. If he's still hitting the third time around, then he must be all right. Cepeda has got it."

Braves catcher Del Crandall agreed, observing: "Cepeda has a big area of plate coverage. He hits a breaking ball better than any rookie I've seen." Added Warren Spahn: "I tried to jam him and he hit a home run to right center!"

By season's end, Giants fans confirmed he was the most popular player on the team. In a poll conducted by the *San Francisco Examiner*, he was named the team's MVP, decisively beating out Willie Mays, 18,701 votes to 11,510.

Among the Elite

In merely his fourth season as a major-leaguer, *before* expansion thinned out the pitching in the National League, Orlando Cepeda enjoyed his most productive major-league season with a league-leading 46 home runs and 142 RBI in 1961.

The feat was obscured by the Roger Maris-Mickey Mantle home run derby in the American League, which already had expanded. But Cepeda's tremendous numbers in 152 games created some buzz about someday surpassing Maris's 61 homers.

"Cepeda undoubtedly is one of the strongest guys in the league," Warren Spahn said. "He just hits the ball nine miles. Even when he hits it on the handle, it goes. He can bust a bat all to pieces and still get a hit, he's so strong."

Spahn obviously was impressed with Cepeda on June 4, 1959, when the second-year slugger drove in seven runs with four hits off teammates Lew Burdette, Juan Pizarro and Carlton Willey. Two of them were homers, one rocketing out of County Stadium.

Robin Roberts also could attest to Cepeda's strength. In an early 1961 game at Connie Mack Stadium, Cepeda hit a ball that left everyone in amazement. It cleared the roof of the second deck and crashed into a soft drink sign nearly 500 feet from the plate.

In the opener of a July 4 doubleheader at Wrigley Field, he knocked in eight runs with five hits, one of them a monster homer off Jim Brewer deep into the center field seats, a drive estimated at more than 500 feet. He added two hits in the second game.

His 40th home run that season came at Candlestick Park against the Dodgers. Sandy Koufax provided the fastball, and

Orlando crushed it and sent it screaming some 420 feet to right-center—a wrongfield homer that would have made a pull hitter envious.

"He has that exceptional power," Hank Sauer said. "You watch how the ball jumps off his bat. It only does that with the good ones. It really jumps. And he can beat Mays to first base. And I've never seen a kid so eager to learn."

Cepeda or McCovey?

Giants managers from Bill Rigney to Herman Franks shared a common problem: How to keep Cepeda and Willie McCovey in the lineup. Both were first basemen—and not at all enemies as has been speculated—and both felt uncomfortable playing out of position, which created some headaches for their skippers.

Rigney, in fact, pointed to Cepeda as a reason for the 1959 collapse that preceded his firing in 1960. The Giants squandered a two-game lead with eight games remaining, aggravating owner Horace Stoneham and dimming the luster of a dazzling Rookie of the Year debut by McCovey.

"Stretch came up, and I talked like a bloody Dutch uncle to get Cepeda to play left field because he could have," Rigney recalled in the mid-70s. "And then I could have had both of them in the lineup. He couldn't do it. He just wouldn't do it. He felt like he was being put down.

"In that small park [Seals Stadium], the fans along first base all loved him. He was The Baby Bull, and he felt he was being displaced. And as hard as I tried, I just couldn't convince him. I ended up having one of them on the bench, whereas if we had both of their bats, it might have given us a lift when we needed it."

By 1966, the Giants finally solved their persistent problem, sending Cepeda to St. Louis for left-hander Ray Sadecki. They were criticized when Cepeda became the MVP for the Cardinals in 1967 and Sadecki turned into a tough-luck loser for the Giants, but if one had to go, the Giants made the right choice.

After they no longer were teammates, Cepeda hit 153 home runs with 598 RBI. In his remaining years with San Francisco, McCovey added 304 homers, 947 RBI and his own MVP award.

A Mental Block

Cepeda's failure to adjust to a different position occurred in 1959, when McCovey broke in with a sensational four-hit game against the Philadelphia Phillies. Rigney asked Cepeda to move to third base, his original position, and it was a horrible experience.

He brooded after making three errors in four games, once hitting a fan in the stands with a throw that sailed over McCovey's head. Then, he was shifted to left field, where his fielding was adequate but his mind set wasn't.

"I just wasn't ready mentally," Cepeda explained. "I know I could have played left field if I put my mind to it, but I was only 21 and very sensitive. It was all pride with me—and ignorance.

"I tried to play left field, and I couldn't do it. My mind wasn't able to do it because I was a good first baseman, and I guess I was too young to realize what was happening. I just wanted to play first base. It started to affect my hitting. It just didn't work out."

Gaylord Perry:
Spit and Polish on the Mound

The Longest Day Launched a New Pitch, 300-win Career

The Longest Day

Gaylord Perry called it "the first spitball victory of my career" when he resorted to doctoring the baseball in a 10-inning relief stint, May 31, 1964, when he finished the Giants' 8-6 victory in 23 innings at Shea Stadium.

It was the second game of a long doubleheader with the New York Mets, and Perry was the fourth pitcher summoned by manager Alvin Dark in the nightcap. He yielded seven hits, struck out nine and walked one.

Perry credits that game with turning his career around. He placed some slippery elm in his mouth to provide more saliva, the movement on his pitches improved dramatically, and Dark shook his hand and placed him in the rotation following the ironman effort.

"The juice in my mouth was slicker than an eel," Perry recalled in his autobiography. "My mouth was watering like a hungry hound's at eating time. Suddenly, I felt like a pitcher again...my confidence came back."

Drool or Deception

Despite the constant commotion over his "hard slider," Perry insisted that he used it far less than batters believed. He came up with the pitch in desperation, learning it from teammate Bob Shaw in 1964 and being encouraged by catcher Tom Haller to use it that fateful day against the Mets.

Gaylord Perry was the master of the spitball. (AP/WWP)

"I was the 11th man on an 11-man staff, and the 12th man was in [Triple-A] Tacoma," Perry explained. "We were out of pitchers that day at Shea Stadium, so it was a good time to use it.

"But after a while, I found out that the motions I went through did more for me than the spitter. Hitters kept worrying about something I didn't do, so it made my other pitches a lot better and I started winning ballgames."

Pass the Mustard

Perry, after admitting he doctored the baseball on occasion, made the following humorous confession long after his retirement:

"I reckon I tried everything on the old apple but salt and pepper and chocolate sauce topping."

The Greatest Start

Perry was the buzz in 1966. On Aug. 20, a five-hit, 6-1 victory over the Atlanta Braves at Candlestick Park improved his record to an incredible 20-2. It was a season when everything seemed to be going right, beginning with a 5-0 record in spring training and including a victory in the All-Star Game.

There was talk about the first 30-win season since Dizzy Dean in 1930, an amazing prospect considering he hadn't made his first start until the Giants' 11th game and was out of action for three weeks when he injured his left ankle sliding into third base.

But following that 20-2 start, the bad luck which was to hound him in 1967-68 suddenly struck Perry down the stretch. He lost his next six decisions and won merely once in the final six weeks as the Giants finished one and one-half games behind the Dodgers.

"What happed after I was 20-2 was that I started losing 2-1 and 4-3," recalled Perry, who actually was off to an even more remarkable 26-2 that season. That's because he was 5-0 in spring training and was the winning pitcher in the All-Star Game.

At the time, he attributed his newfound success to his "hard slider," but hitters had another name for the slippery, sinking baseball, as Eddie Mathews summed up: "All that slider talk is a bunch of bunk. Perry is the pitcher he is today because he's learned to control his spitter."

Hassling the Hammer

Hank Aaron similarly was frustrated by Perry's decoying, so the pitcher loved playing mind games with "The Hammer." He would tug the bill of his cap, and Aaron would step out of the box, thinking Perry was loading up.

In a 1967 game against the Atlanta Braves, this went on a few times, and Aaron yelled for Perry "to throw that blankety-blank and I'll take it outta here!" Instead of throwing his famous "sinker," Perry struck out Aaron with a slow, roundhouse curve.

"Hank looked down at the plate," Perry recalled, "and splashed it with a wad of spit that would have lasted me three innings.

"Then he turned to [umpire] Doug Harvey and said, 'Why don't you just let him carry a bucket of water out there?' I was hurt. That pitch was as dry as a Baptist wedding."

Marathon Man

Perry, who went on to win 300 games, demonstrated his durability in 1967 with 16 shutout innings against the Cincinnati Reds at Crosley Field, Sept. 1. But unlike teammate Juan Marichal, who posted a 16-inning shutout in 1963, Perry had nothing to show for it but a tired arm.

It was the longest night game in major-league history, lasting five hours and 40 minutes. The Giants were 1-0 winners when Dick Groat walked with the bases loaded in the 21st inning. Frank Linzy replaced Perry and worked five shutout innings for the win.

"[Manager] Herman Franks asked me in the 14th inning how I felt, and I told him I wanted to stay on," Perry said. "But I'd had it after the 16th. My right arm was so tired, I couldn't lift it.

"Yes, that was one of my better games, but it wasn't that big a deal to pitch a lot of innings in those days. I remember pitching 17 innings in the minors. I always wanted to finish what I started. There wasn't as much emphasis on relief pitching like there is today."

Perry had one complaint after the marathon concluded.

"No room service," he quipped.

Comic Relief

Gaylord Perry's famous spitter elicited some humorous remarks from frustrated hitters, according to his controversial autobiography, *Me and the Spitter*. One of the best came from Pete Rose.

In his first 1968 start against the Reds, Perry was pitching to Rose in Cincinnati. On the very first pitch to Charlie Hustle, Perry loaded up and fired a pitch that Rose missed by one foot, and Pete took his anger out on the plate umpire.

Perry then resorted to his decoy after having Rose thinking about a greaseball, so he struck him out on change-ups. He protested so loudly that the umpire threw him out of the game, whereby Perry recalled the following exchange:

"Hey, Perry, where do you keep your dip stick?" Rose asked.

"What do you mean?" Perry replied.

"How else will you know when your cap needs an oil change?"

No-Hitting the Champs

Perry regarded it as the best game he ever pitched when he fired a 1-0 no-hitter against the pennant-winning St. Louis Cardinals at Candlestick Park, Sept. 17, 1968. Some suggested it was tainted because the Cardinals were a little groggy from a championship celebration the previous night.

But Perry was masterful, claiming "there was nothing close to a hit that day," and was rewarded when light-hitting Ron Hunt homered off Bob Gibson with one out in the first inning for the game's only run before a small crowd of 9,546.

"I was very excited about it because the Cardinals were the best, and there was nothing close to a hit that day," said Perry, who struck out nine and walked two. The next day, Ray Washburn exacted some revenge when he threw a 2-0 no-hitter against the Giants for the first back-to-back no-nos in history.

What is often forgotten is that Perry came close to pitching two no-hitters that season. On Aug. 26, against the Chicago Cubs at Candlestick Park, the only hit off him was a seventh-inning single by Glenn Beckert.

"When I got to the seventh against the Cardinals, I couldn't help thinking of Beckert," Perry conceded. "The no-hitter was a special thrill because it came so soon after the one-hitter, and I had a two-hitter at Chicago just before that, so I was pitching well."

Imagine if He Were Lucky

Perry finished a Hall of Fame career with 308 victories—134 as a Giant—and he could have had many more were it not for a sluggish start and the reputation as a tough-luck loser during his years in San Francisco. In fact, he was a mere 24-30 after four seasons with the club.

In 1967, for instance, he posted a 2.61 ERA and had merely a 15-17 record to show for it, losing by one run nine times, including five 2-1 defeats. Against the champion Cardinals that year, he sported a 2.23 ERA and an 0-5 record.

Perry defeated the Cardinals in 1968, throwing a no-hitter against them, but he didn't have long to savor the gem because St. Louis's Ray Washburn no-hit the Giants the next day. That season, Gaylord was 16-15 with a 2.44 ERA, receiving fewer than two runs of support in 11 defeats.

"You can't let it stay in your mind," he said of his tough luck. "It's easy to get upset, but if you stay upset you're never going to win a ballgame. You've got to stay positive, keep trying to do better.

"Yes, I had a lot of close losses in those days. I seemed to always draw the opponents' best pitcher because they seldom were matched with Juan (Marichal). All those close games made me a better pitcher. I *had* to bear down."

Shooting for the Moon

Perry was such a dismal hitter when he first joined the Giants that manager Alvin Dark boldly predicted: "There will be a man on the moon before he hits a home run."

On July 20, 1969, some 20 minutes after The Eagle made a successful lunar landing, Perry connected off Claude Osteen of the Dodgers for his first major-league home run.

Protecting the Perfect Bat

Joe Torre was an outstanding hitter during his playing days, but one of the pitchers he didn't enjoy facing was Gaylord Perry, because he was concerned about what might happen to one of his prized bats.

"Gaylord killed me," Torre said. "He'd always jam me. I remember having a bat that was just perfect. It had a real wide grain and I'd been going good with it for about two months. Well, he was pitching against us one day and I didn't want to use that bat, fearing he'd jam me and crack the handle.

"So I borrowed someone else's bat. But I didn't realize that Jose Cardenal picked up my bat, used it and broke it. He had the same idea. He didn't want Gaylord breaking his favorite bat, either."

That'll Cost You, Kid

When Steve Stone was a rookie with the Giants in 1971, Perry approached him and said, "You can really benefit from *my* pitch because you throw hard over the top and it would be a natural for you," referring to his fabled spitter.

"I was flattered that he would come up to me and offer his time," Stone recalled, "so I told Gaylord, 'Great, when do we start?'

"As soon as you bring me $3,000," came Perry's prompt reply.

"But Gaylord, I only make $13,000 and take home about $8.5, so my wife and I barely make ends meet," Stone said. "We can't afford to do that."

"Steve, you're thinking short-term," Perry answered. "You have to think about the long-term benefits. When you can afford it, we'll talk."

Stone, contending veterans were supposed to teach youngsters the ropes out of duty, never accepted Perry's offer. But he does have one thing in common with the Hall of Famer—each was a Cy Young Award winner after leaving the Giants.

What Were They Thinking?

For some reason, blundering Giants management had the notion that "Sudden" Sam McDowell had a better future than Gaylord Perry, so they consummated a trade with the Cleveland Indians, Nov. 29, 1971, and also included infielder Frank Duffy so they could get McDowell, who was known for his boozing as much as his blazer.

That, of course, would not have been regarded as a detriment by owner Horace Stoneham, who appeased manager Charlie Fox with the controversial trade. While McDowell was a combined 11-10 in his 11/2 San Francisco seasons before being sold to the Yankees, June 7, 1973, Perry won 24 games and a Cy Young Award in 1972.

"If it were up to me, I'd have finished my career with the Giants," Perry said prior to his Hall of Fame induction. "It was Charlie Fox's idea because he really wanted Sam McDowell. If he tells you otherwise, he's a liar."

What They'd Say About Gay

"Gaylord was an outstanding competitor. He'd beat you any way he could. He'd knock you down when he had to. He'd load it up when he had to. Whatever it took. He'd work on your mind. I remember thinking about the spitter and taking three fastballs right down the middle. He definitely played mind games with you."

—*Lou Piniella*

"It seemed like you were always 0-2 against Gaylord. Players all knew he threw it [spitter or greaseball], but he had you worrying about it so much, he had you where he wanted you. And he was always talking to you, anything to disract you."

—*Joe Torre*

"I'd get some hits off him, and then he'd tell me he couldn't even get me out in the minors. I didn't remember facing him in the minors, but he always did things to get your mind working. Gaylord's spitter was very subtle, breaking just enough to throw you off. You knew what it was, but you couldn't hit it real good."

—*Mike Shannon*

"He was an unbelievable competitor. He'd find a way to beat you. He could beat you psychologically with his ability to strike fear in a hitter. It seemed like he kept his team in the game all the time."

—*Ozzie Smith*

"He got you so aware of what he was doing with the ball, you lost sight of how much stuff he had. I remember that puffball before they outlawed it. He'd get the resin all over it, and it looked like it was coming out of a cloud on the way to the plate."

—*Dusty Baker*

"Gaylord was tough to hit, with or without the spitter. He went to it when he was in trouble, but he had good stuff anyway. He was as tough to face as [Juan] Marichal, and they complemented each other."

—Ron Fairly

"He had a habit of picking up the resin bag and tossing it up and down so you'd take your mind off his pitching. And then he'd take that resin bag and get that stuff all over the ball. When it came to the plate, it looked like an exploding fastball, like there was smoke coming from it."

—Joe Morgan

Will Clark:
New Giants Hero

"The Thrill" Powers the Humm-Babies

A Flair for Dramatics

Will Clark didn't take long to make an impact as a pro. Playing his first game in the Giants' farm system, June 21, 1985, at Class-A Fresno, he demonstrated that adjusting from aluminum bats to wood wouldn't be a major problem.

On his first professional swing, against Jeff Rojas of Visalia, Clark belted a two-run homer over the left field fence at John Euless Park in Fresno. He later added a second home run and finished with two hits and four RBI in a 14-1 rout.

And Clark was in a comfort zone for openers. Right-hander Jeff Brantley, a teammate at Mississippi State and the Giants' sixth-round draft choice, also made his pro debut and was the winning pitcher.

Clark batted .309 with 10 homers in 65 games with Fresno that season, and .487 with three homers in 10 instructional league games. In his first spring training exhibition with the Giants, he homered again, and on March 23 was told he was the Giants' first baseman. The best was yet to come.

Can You Top This?

Willie McCovey's four-hit debut against Robin Roberts in 1959 and Bobby Bonds's first-game grand slam homer against the Dodgers in 1968 were regarded as the most impressive beginnings in San Francisco history. They were joined in magnitude when Will Clark stepped to the plate at the Astrodome, April 8, 1986.

Among the 23,000-plus in attendance Opening Day was a large contingent of Clark's family and friends from New Orleans, and he was a bit of a showoff. On his first major-league swing, Clark sent a high Nolan Ryan change-up soaring some 420 feet and into the center field seats for a 1-0 Giants lead in the first inning.

"As I was going to second," Clark recalled following the 8-3 victory over the Houston Astros, "I just said to myself, 'Good, it's 1-0.' Then I realized I had hit it off Nolan Ryan, and that it was my first big-league at-bat. You have to smile about something like that."

His teammates were equally amazed over Clark's impersonation of Roy Hobbs. This kid was supposed to be good, but nobody knew how good. As he rounded second, Clark realized what he'd done and broke out with a huge grin. He looked up toward his family after crossing the plate and practically floated into the dugout.

"He tried to act like he wasn't happy, but he was ready to do cartwheels from home plate to the dugout," said teammate Bob Brenly, who soon nicknamed the brash rookie Will the Thrill.

Déjà vu in Week Two

Before Barry Bonds became the darling of the home crowds with a string of memorable home runs that appeased Giants fans, Will Clark demonstrated a similar penchant for rising to the occasion. And it didn't take long. He homered on his first pro swing in Fresno, in his first exhibition and in his major-league debut.

One week after connecting against Nolan Ryan in Houston, the Giants hosted the Astros in the home opener, April 15, 1986, and 46,638 showed up at Candlestick Park to watch Vida Blue shoot for his 200th major-league victory and Clark make his home debut, not necessarily in order of importance to the curious crowd.

Phil Garner's three-run homer in the first inning and solo homers by Garner and Kevin Bass in the third gave the Astros a quick 5-0 lead off Blue, but the crowd wasn't totally disappointed.

In the fifth inning, rookie Robby Thompson walked and Clark connected on a 2-2 Bob Knepper pitch and sent a towering fly over the right field fence.

"It was sweet," Clark conceded following the 8-3 defeat and his three-hit home debut. "They're leaving the ball over the plate, and when they do that I'm supposed to hit it. Hitting is a matter of putting the meat part of the bat on the ball—that's something I excel at."

Will the Thrill

Teammate Bob Brenly is credited with giving Will Clark his nickname, "Will the Thrill." It didn't take long for the veteran catcher to recognize that the rookie first baseman was something special, especially after his Opening Day home runs in Houston and San Francisco.

"It was just one of those things that seemed to roll off the tongue," Brenly said of the origin of the apt moniker. "There are some players that just have an aura about them. You could tell right away that Will was one of those kind of guys.

"He didn't have to say or do anything. He was confident before he knew what he was confident about. He had a knack for knowing when everybody was looking at him to do something. Those were the situations where he seemed to thrive."

It was immediately obvious that Clark didn't lack confidence. When asked about his quick start, Clark merely shrugged and said: "When I went to spring training, I wasn't thinking that I'd be going back to [Triple-A] Phoenix."

Of course, he didn't, instead launching a career that would help the Giants return to prominence. Soon, Clark had the reputation to match his swagger. A sign above his locker in spring training read: "Once you realize I'm God, we'll get along fine."

Success Comes Quickly

Will Clark embarrassed himself by, and later apologized for, becoming overwhelmed by the Giants' division-clinching victory in 1987, his first full season as a major leaguer. "I've waited so long for this!" a champagne-drenched Clark shrieked on television, making those wince who knew it was 16 years between titles for the club.

However, that was the only time the Thrill embarrassed himself during a season in which he batted .308 with a career-high 35 home runs and added a .360 average in the NLCS. Clark thereby became the first Giant with a .300 average and 30 homers since Willie McCovey was the MVP in 1969.

"He's a hitter who comes along about once in a decade," manager Roger Craig said during a season in which Clark tied a club record shared by Willie Mays, Orlando Cepeda and McCovey with an RBI in nine straight games and had three game-winning homers on the Giants' final at-bats.

Clark Becomes No. 1

Players like Barry Bonds and Mark McGwire went on to more success from Will Clark's rookies class, but after the first few years of their careers, Clark's consistency and success placed him in a class of his own. That was verified on Feb. 22, 1990, when a four-year, $15-million contract made him the game's highest-paid player ever.

"He plays like a Hall of Famer, and he should be paid like one," general manager Al Rosen said of the megabucks deal. "Will Clark is the premier player in the game today and earns every cent."

Rosen was criticized by rival clubs for the spending spree, but Clark clearly was at the top of his game. In 1989, he became the first Giant to lead the All-Star Game voting, batted .333 for the NL champions and set a record with a .650 batting average in the NLCS against the Chicago Cubs, collecting the pennant-winning hit.

Will Clark demonstrates the sweet swing that helped earn him the nickname "Will the Thrill." (AP/WWP)

Will Warms Up

The 1993 Giants hit a wall in early September, losing eight in a row and their division lead before regrouping to go 14-3 down the stretch. But their chances didn't look good on Sept. 24, against the San Diego Padres at Candlestick Park, where a Trevor Hoffman fastball shattered Robby Thompson's left cheekbone leading off the eighth inning.

After Thompson was helped off the field, Will Clark singled on Hoffman's next pitch, sending pinch-runner Mike Benjamin to third. Matt Williams's sacrifice fly created a 2-2 tie, and it stayed that way until the bottom of the 10th. Gene Harris retired the first two Giants, but his first pitch to Clark sailed over the fence for a 3-2 victory.

It was Clark's first home run since Aug. 5, and it began a string of dramatic hits down the stretch for "The Thrill" in his final games with the Giants. More importantly, his clutch homers slashed the Braves' division lead to one and one-half games.

In his final seven games with the Giants, Clark went out with a flurry. He batted .500, 14 for 28, including two four-hit games in the final series with the Dodgers. The Thrill was going, but he wasn't gone.

What They Said About Clark

"If you were a kid, you'd look at Will and try to copy him. They'll have to consider him for Rookie of the Year, but he doesn't look like one. He looks like he's been around for a while."
—Tony Gwynn in 1986

"I hesitate to ever say it, but Will reminds me of Stan Musial. "He's quick to adjust to pitchers, and he has great hands in the field."
—Manager Roger Craig in 1986

"He's the best pure hitter I've seen come along in a long time—a natural hitter."
—*Jim Lefebvre*

"He comes off as cocky to some people, but there's no questioning his ability. He's a natural. He's going through what I did when you come up heralded as a potential superstar and have to meet the high expectations of everyone else."
—*Chili Davis*

"There's no question Will and Andres Galarraga are the next two standouts at first base. I don't see cockiness in him. I call it youthful exuberance. You like to see such enthusiasm from players."
—*Keith Hernandez*

"I knew I could get to Will. I introduced him to a lot of stuff he was going to run into as a major-leaguer. I wanted to test him, but I never doubted his ability. He's a left-handed hitter with a sweet swing made to order for Candlestick."
—*Jeffrey Leonard*

"Will is a great hitter, but what I like best about him is his attitude. He slides into second base hard. He comes to play. He reminds me of myself."
—*Pete Rose*

"There's something about him that all the great players have. It's an extra pressure they place on themselves to excel every day. And you can't teach a swing like his. He has tremendous bat speed and reactions, so the ball just jumps off his bat."
—*Chris Speier*

"Will's star quality is obvious because of his attitude. He gets mad when he doesn't do well, but he doesn't get discouraged."
—*Dusty Baker*

"Of the young players who have come up the last three or four years, Will is probably as good a hitter as we've seen. You have to like the way he adjusts. Most young hitters are mistake hitters, not great hitters. Will is a great hitter, a pure hitter."

—*Nolan Ryan*

"It seems like he thrives on pressure situations, wanting to be at the plate with men on base and the game on the line. He adjusts very well. He's willing to take what they [pitchers] give, and he'll use the whole field."

—*Rick Reuschel*

"He might go 0 for 12, but he still has such a tremendous impact. I've played with some impact players, but Will is different. He has impact whether he's playing well or not. There's just such a force about him, more than anybody I've ever played with."

—*Bob Knepper*

Barry Bonds:
No Giant Ever Did It Better

Former Candlestick Kid Makes
Pac Bell a Personal Playground

A Candlestick Kid

When Barry Bonds was between the ages of four and 10, his father Bobby was a star with the Giants, so there were frequent trips to Candlestick Park to watch baseball and play around the clubhouse. Like many youngsters, he was attracted to Willie Mays, his godfather.

"Barry was a kid about five when I got him," Mays recalled. "He used to come in my locker, eat all my chewing gum and play with my glove. I would take him out in center field and play catch with him all the time. This went on daily when we were home.

"He got to know me a little better than he did everybody else, and whenever he had problems, he would come to me for guidance. His mother would drop him off at my locker. Barry learned a lot by hanging around the clubhouse."

Bonds concurred, speaking fondly of the days when he literally learned in the lap of the master.

"I'll never forget it as long as I live," he said of his youth at The Stick. "I used to climb to the top of the lockers and hide Willie's glove from him—a great experience."

Spurning the Giants

After batting .467 as a senior at Serra High, Barry Bonds had an opportunity to become one of those rare players to spend his entire career with one team. His beloved Giants drafted him in

Barry Bonds hit his 600th career home run in 2002.
(Photo courtesy of the San Francisco Giants)

1982, and there is a misconception that a contract hassle between his father, Bobby Bonds, and the club management kept him from turning pro.

It was widely circulated that a $5,000 difference in what the Bondses were asking and what the Giants were offering made him elect an Arizona State University scholarship instead. There was even talk that Frank Robinson, then the Giants' manager, was willing to pay the $5,000 to have Bobby's boy sign a contract.

"The fact is that I wanted to go to school," Barry disclosed many years later. "Dad figured what a college education was worth, and the Giants didn't want to pay that much, but it really wouldn't have mattered. Frank's gesture was nice, but it was after the fact. I was going to school."

The decision prevented Barry from perhaps being a Giant for life, but it didn't hinder his development. In three seasons at ASU, Bonds batted .347 with 45 homers and 175 RBI, set a College World Series record with seven straight hits as a sophomore and was an All-American in 1985 before signing with the Pittsburgh Pirates as a first-rounder.

The Cornerstone

When Peter Magowan headed the investors' group that purchased the Giants, a power-hitting left fielder who batted from the left side was a top priority. Barry Bonds wasn't necessarily the first choice, but obviously the best solution.

"David Justice and Larry Walker came to mind," Magowan conceded. "But they weren't free agents, and they would have cost us a player or two. So Barry was the obvious choice.

"We hadn't completed the purchase, but I sought out six general managers and asked them what what the Giants needed most. I thought they might say a pitching ace, but they all said a power-hitting left fielder who bats left-handed."

When Bonds was signed to a six-year contract worth $43.75 million—baseball's richest deal at the time—Magowan proved prophetic in estimating the impact Bonds would have on the rejuvenated club.

"The 49ers were playing at home, and Mario Lemieux [Penguins] and Michael Jordan [Bulls] were in town, and we were the ones people were talking about," Magowan recalled. "He's going to have a tremendous impact. He's going to make everyone better."

Dazzling Debut

Barry Bonds couldn't have picked a better time to have his finest major-league season. Justifying ownership's faith in making him baseball's highest-paid player, his 1993 debut with the Giants was a smash hit on all fronts, including 103 victories, a third MVP award in four years and career highs in batting (.336), homers (46) and RBI (123).

Bonds wasted little time in supplanting Will Clark as the main man in the Giants' attack. On Opening Day in St. Louis, his seventh-inning sacrifice fly produced a 2-1 victory. He homered in his second game and again on his first Giants at-bat on Opening Day at Candlestick Park before 56,689 in a 4-3 victory over the Florida Marlins.

His opening month with the Giants was an accurate barometer of what was to come. He batted .431 with seven homers and 25 RBI as the National League Player of the Month for April. Bonds was the leading vote-getter with 3,074,603 in the All-Star balloting and finished the season as strong as he started it.

As the Giants battled the Atlanta Braves down the stretch, Bonds enjoyed a monster game, Oct. 1, at Dodger Stadium. His two three-run homers and a double produced a career-high seven RBI in an 8-7 victory. His .336 was the highest average ever by a Giant playing home games at The Stick, and his .677 slugging percentage set the franchise record.

"This MVP is the best because I came home," Bonds said after receiving 24 of 28 first-place votes and finishing with 372 points in the baseball writers' poll. Len Dykstra of the Philadelphia Phillies was a distant second with 267 points.

The 400-400 Club

On Aug. 23, 1998, Mark McGwire and Sammy Sosa clearly were the talk of baseball. That day, McGwire hit his 53rd home run and Sammy Sosa belted a pair for a total of 51. The Great Home Run Race was heating up.

So was Barry Bonds. That same day in Miami, the Giants' superslugger homered with one on off Kirt Ojala in the third inning of a 10-5 victory over the Florida Marlins and former manager Jim Leyland. It was the 400th of his career and made him the first member of the exclusive 400-400 Club. (He had 438 stolen bases).

"This is a big accomplishment, but it's nothing compared to what McGwire and Sosa are doing," Bonds said. "Look around. I have nine writers here for this occasion. Mac's had 250. He's got to be going nuts getting the same questions every day.

"Two guys doing what they're doing—what's the chances of that? What I did is more about staying healthy and playing for a long time. What they're doing is incredible. The fact two players might do it [60 homers] the same year, that's huge."

A few years later, Bonds would have the same experience as McGwire and Sosa, but he underestimated his power and overestimated his speed when asked about 500-500.

"It's going to be a little tough, but I'm almost halfway there in steals—I can do that," said Bonds, who completed the 2002 season with 613 home runs and 493 stolen bases.

The Greatest Snub

Ever since Barry Bonds joined the Giants in 1993, he had been compared with Ken Griffey Jr. There was a common bond because both were the sons of former major-leaguers, both hit a lot of home runs and both were gifted athletes in all phases of the game.

What bothered Bonds is that it turned into a personality contest, with Junior receiving more support because he had a better image. This seemed evident in 2000 when Griffey was named a member of the All-Century Team while Bonds was excluded from the 100 finalists—even though he was the Player of the Decade.

Curiously, when Bonds shattered major-league records in 2001-2002, he was placed on a pedestal alongside Babe Ruth, Willie Mays and Hank Aaron as perhaps the greatest player ever. It's amazing what 73 home runs and a .370 batting average can do to change perceptions.

"Junior is a great player, a hell of a player, and he's going to excite people for the next decade," Bonds said in 1996. "He's going to put up numbers only the great players put up. But until that time comes, he has to go step by step, like everybody else. Junior hasn't done what I've done. I've got statistics in my book that he hasn't touched yet."

Still hasn't. Bonds wasn't being malicious, but he was extremely accurate. Ever since becoming a National Leaguer with the Cincinnati Reds in 2000, Griffey was bogged down by injuries and no longer was regarded among the elite. And at last count (through 2002), he had one MVP award to Bonds's five.

"He's been the best player in the game for the last 15 years, hands down," Junior said in 2001. "Just look at what this guy has done. It's almost like they've taken him for granted, not paying any attention to him until now. He's got the respect of everybody in the game."

A False Impression

Most first-time visitors to Pacific Bell Park think it's a power hitter's paradise, and Barry Bonds was no exception. During a preview of the new ballpark, Jan. 21, 2000, Bonds glanced at the 309-foot distance down the right field line and salivated.

Then he and teammates Jeff Kent, J. T. Snow, Bill Mueller and Rich Aurilia took batting practice on a dirt field with coaches doing the pitching. Bonds hit the unofficial first "homer," driving balls over the wall in right and center.

"Right field does seem close," Bonds said after his first cuts in the new yard. "And I hit a ball to right center that I didn't think would go out, but it did. The ballpark is gorgeous. It's going to be very exciting for the fans."

Bonds was correct on his last observation, and while he continued to flourish as a home run hitter at Pac Bell, it became a difficult park for most hitters. Snow made a more accurate observation following that batting session.

"People will know it's a short fence in right," he said, "but the wall isn't only eight or 10 feet high. Pitchers will work left-handed hitters outside, and if they pitch you away, you've got to hit it the other way. A few swings today doesn't tell you how the park will play."

Barry Bounces Back

Injuries contributed greatly to Barry Bonds's worst season as a Giant in 1999. He played in only 102 games, batted .262 and had "only" 34 home runs and 83 RBI, certainly short by his standards. In 2000, however, there were early indications that the old Barry was back.

During the Chicago Cubs' first visit to Pacific Bell Park for a series in May, slugger Sammy Sosa had a particularly encouraging batting practice before making a bold prediction that turned out to be not nearly as far-fetched as it sounded.

"Barry is going to hit 80 home runs, no doubt," said Sosa, who had 15 home runs to Bonds's 19 at the time. "This right field fence is made for him."

Bonds would have to wait one year to nearly fulfill Sosa's prophecy and make home run history, but 2000 was a jump start. He finished the season with a career-high 49 home runs in 143 games and 480 at-bats, but he wasn't convinced.

"I'm almost 36 now, so I'm not getting caught up in any home run race stuff," Bonds said after a 2000 stretch in which he blasted 14 home runs in 21 games. "I just don't spend much time analyzing stuff like that. I've never hit 50 in my life, but anything's possible."

Fairly prophetic himself.

The Impossible Dream

As the Giants prepared to open a series with the Dodgers on April 17, 2001, at Pacific Bell Park, Barry Bonds was on the threshold of 500 home runs, and he couldn't believe it.

"You never dream of being in a position to do certain things," Bonds said. "I just never thought it was possible or reachable—and the next thing you know, you're knocking on the door."

The knock was answered with the Giants trailing 2-1 in the bottom of the eighth. Rich Aurilia led off with a triple, and Bonds followed by sending a 2-0 Terry Adams slider deep into the deep at McCovey Cove, an estimated 417-footer.

"I've got to thank my parents for having me," an emotional Bonds addressed the 41,059 in attendance during lengthy ceremonies that disturbed the Dodgers, "and I want to thank Willie Mays and Willie McCovey for being here."

Mays became the 17th player in the 500 Club, joining the two Willies. Following the 3-2 victory, Mays recalled a humbled Bonds at home plate after the historic homer: "When I touched him, he was still shaking. I think he now realizes what history is all about. He really appreciated it."

Added Bonds: "It's a weight lifted off my chest. Hitting it into McCovey Cove is the ultimate. That made it better."

A Wild Atlanta Weekend

Barry Bonds's record 2001 home run chase really took off at Turner Field, when he hit six home runs in a three-game series against the vaunted Atlanta Braves' pitching staff on May 18-20. He hit one in the opener, cranked out three in the second game, and capped his explosive weekend with a pair in the Sunday finale.

"I'm going to enjoy this ride as long as I can, but it's still going to end up like it always has," said Bonds, meaning he likely would finish with between 40 and 50 home runs, his norm. "Atlanta surprised me. I don't hit many balls off them."

It didn't stop there. Bonds connected off Curt Schilling at Bank One Ballpark the next night and homered off Russ Springer in the second game of the Arizona Diamondbacks' series. That made it nine home runs in six consecutive games, a National League record.

"I've seen Barry hit a lot of homers the last five years, but never so many in a row—it's amazing," Rich Aurilia said. Added J. T. Snow: "I don't know if you can come to expect it of him, but on the other hand, you know he's the one guy who can do it. I'd never seen anything like it—pretty impressive."

Halfway There

When Barry Bonds entered the All-Star break with 39 home runs, the most ever hit at that juncture, the media crush had already started. But Bonds sincerely played down the record pursuit and expressed doubts that Mark McGwire's 70 home runs could be reached. McGwire was in agreement.

"Mark is the big man, the home run man," Bonds insisted. "He's averaged 50 home runs for the last four or five years, and I've never even hit 50. He's been hitting home runs ever since he was born, and I've had to learn how to hit them. He hits it 520 feet when he's tired. He can miss and it goes 450 feet.

"I don't think about McGwire's record. I don't want McGwire's record. I won't care if I don't get it. I don't need personal records. I have quite a few of those. I want a World Series ring. Mac's home run record is not in jeopardy."

McGwire, not demeaning Bonds's hot start, also was realistic, observing: "It's fantastic, an outstading year so far. What he's doing right now is unbelievable, incredible. But wait till someone gets 60 by September, and you've got a story.

"It's tougher now because once you get to 60, you've got to hit 11 more. The pressure will be unbelievable. I felt it every day and overcame it. I'm still trying to decipher what happened that year [1998]. It's difficult to repeat in the second half what you've done in the first half."

Triumph and Tragedy

Barry Bonds was giddy on Sept. 9, 2001 at Coors Field, and it wasn't because of the thin air. His Rocky Mountain high was the result of three prodigious home runs that boosted his total to 63 and made him the most prolific single-season left-handed slugger in history, passing Roger Maris.

The three home runs travelled a combined 1,243 feet and gave him 32 on the road, tying a major-league record shared by Babe Ruth and Mark McGwire. It left him with 18 games remaining to catch McGwire for the single-season record.

"That was a lot of fun," Bonds said following the 9-4 victory over the Colorado Rockies, thanks to his 11th-inning homer. "I've been in disbelief for a lot of things I've done this year. Everything is unreal right now."

Teammate Jeff Kent added: "It's his time—let him enjoy it. I've never seen Barry be such a dominating player as he is now. To hit the ball like he has this year, it's incredible. How do you top it? He can do anything he wants to do."

The Giants then took a charter flight to Houston for an off day, and the elation soon turned to tears. Bonds's record pursuit seemed so insignificant on Sept. 11, when the terrorist attack placed everything but grief on hold. It would be another week before Barry and baseball would provide a welcome diversion.

Big Mac On Target

Mark McGwire's specialty was hitting tape-measure home runs, but he wasn't too bad as a prognosticator, either. While Barry Bonds was chasing his record in the final stages of the 2001 season, Big Mac virtually called the shot on Sept. 28.

"I've told guys [teammates] that I'm calling 72 or 73," McGwire told the *St. Louis Post-Dispatch*. "He's got a very, very, very, very, very, very, very good chance at breaking the record— he's phenomenal.

"He's pretty much doing it routinely. His pace is unbelievable. He's totally blown away what I did. Even if the year ended today, his home runs per at-bat [ratio] is just unbelievable. He's also taken a lot of days off, and on those days, he doesn't pinch hit."

Shortly after McGwire's astute prediction, Bonds hit his 68th home run against the Padres at Pacific Bell Park. No. 69 came the next day, before the Giants travelled to Houston, where Astros pitchers were reluctant to pitch to him.

A Blastoff in Houston

Houston Astros manager Larry Dierker and his pitchers were booed by partisan fans and criticized by the local media for avoiding Barry Bonds in the first two games of a series at Enron Field, Oct. 2-4. Barry's 10-year-old daughter, Shikari, provided some comic relief while sitting in the stands.

She held up a sign, "Please pitch to our Daddy."

Then she hoisted a second sign, "Give our Daddy a chance." But the walks persisted until his final at-bat, in the ninth inning of his final road game of the season. With rookie left-hander Wilfredo Rodriguez pitching, Bonds sent a 454-foot bolt into the upper deck on a 1-1 fastball.

The wait was over. Bonds had tied Mark McGwire with No. 70, triggering a wild celebration at home plate as jubilant teammates poured out of the dugout to meet him. A record crowd of 43,734, there to observe history, cheered loudly during two curtain calls.

"We're riding on an adrenaline rush because of Barry," Jeff Kent said following a 10-2 romp and a series sweep that kept the Giants in the race with three games remaining. "It's been an emotional ride for Barry, one we've been watching with amazement."

Bonds, who was walked eight times in the three games before connecting, paid tribute to the man he caught with one mighty swing.

"To me, it's an honor to share this with Mac," Bonds said. "He put the home run record where it is, and I will always respect that. I just feel proud to be on the same level with Mark. I just feel really proud. I don't know how else to explain it."

A Bittersweet Bash

The Giants were celebrating a man and lamenting a loss, making it an extremely bittersweet night at Pacific Bell Park, Oct. 5, 2001. It was the opener of a final weekend series and 41,730 jammed into the ballpark to watch Barry Bonds make history and the Giants to stay in the race.

They got half their wish. With two out and none on in the bottom of the first inning, Bonds sent a 1-0 Chan Ho Park fastball screaming some 442 feet to right center for his 71st home run, and the crowd went wild. So did the Giants, who rushed to the plate for hugs and high fives.

For an encore, Bonds led off the third by blasting a 1-1 Park pitch to left-center for No. 72. The only thing missing was a victory. The Dodgers gladly spoiled the party with an 11-10 victory that eliminated the Giants from the playoff picture.

What made the scene surreal was the mix of emotions at the end of a four-hour, 27-minute game. Ceremonies were held on the field past midnight as a tearful Bonds thanked the fans for their support. But many Giants were devastated by the defeat and weren't in a mood to celebrate.

"A lot of us didn't want to be here," Jeff Kent said the morning after. "We were worn out. All of us were happy for Barry and to someday be able to look back and say we were part of it. But it was a tough night. I felt sorry for Barry—to have such a great season and not win."

An exhausted Bonds rested the next day, and in the first inning of what could have been his final game with the Giants, he lofted a Dennis Springer knuckler over the right field arcade seats for No. 73. He also finished the season with 177 walks and an .863 slugging percentage.

Barry Bonds watches his 71ˢᵗ home run fly into the seats at Pac Bell Park.
(Photo courtesy of the San Francisco Giants)

"It seems Babe ain't going to have many records, is he?" manager Dusty Baker said. Bonds viewed the home run off a knuckler as an appropriate ending to a season even he found difficult to believe.

"I was in shock," Bonds said. "Chances of hitting a homer against a guy who throws that slow are slim. When I did it, I just said, 'What else can you give me, God?—enough is enough.'

"I thought I had a pretty good shot [at the record] when I hit three in Colorado. That got me to 63, but then I had my doubts when I got to Houston this week. If I got stuck on 69 before we played the Dodgers, it would have been tough. When I tied it, I felt relieved."

Betting on Bonds

Shawon Dunston didn't gamble on baseball games, but he bet on Barry Bonds and won a new luxury automobile at the end of the 2001 season. The wager was made after Bonds hit six home runs in a three-game series at Atlanta's Turner Field, May 18-20.

"We were stretching with the guys before a game, and Shawon told me I'd hit 71 home runs —I thought he was crazy," said Bonds, who had 22 homers in 43 games at the time.

And Dunston wasn't kidding about his bold prediction, explaining: "I was serious. You don't go into Atlanta and hit six home runs, not against that pitching staff. Nobody knew he'd hit 70, but you knew this was different. Barry was hitting homers, and we were trying to hit singles."

Bonds made good on the bet as soon as he passed Mark McGwire, announcing that the keys to a $100,000 Mercedes-Benz CL500 would soon be in Dunston's possession.

Nobody bet Bonds he would hit .370 in 2002.

More of the Same

Armed with an unprecedented fourth MVP award and a new five-year contract that assured he would conclude his career with the Giants, Bonds opened the 2002 season in the same manner as he concluded his dynamic 2001—by devastating Dodgers pitching with some remarkable slugging.

On Opening Day at Dodger Stadium, April 2, 2002, he homered off Kevin Brown and Omar Daal to power a 9-2 victory. The next night, it was deja vu all over again. Bonds connected off Hideo Nomo and Terry Mulholland in a 12-0 rout, giving him four in the first two games of the season.

"The more I watch him and reflect on what he's done over the course of his career, you can make a case that he's arguably the greatest who ever played the game," Dodgers manager Jim Tracy said.

Added Dusty Baker: "He picked up where he left off last year, and that's what the greats do. Michael Jordan, Mario Lemieux, Wayne Gretzky—that's what they do, and that's why they're called superstars. It's awesome. It's unbelievable. You just accept it and be thankful for it."

He Got His Wish

It wasn't the World Series, but Barry Bonds finally got his wish to play in Yankee Stadium in an interleague series, June 7-9, and he made the most of it. Batting against left-hander Ted Lilly in the first inning of the second game, he hit a three-run homer 17 rows into the upper deck, triggering a 4-3 victory.

"He was built to play here," said Yankees first baseman Jason Giambi, who admired the blast along with the 56,194 in attendance. The bolt into the blue (seats) conservatively was estimated at 385 feet, but it seemed to be hit much harder and farther.

"I think that's what they [fans] wanted to see," Bonds said. "It feels great to hit a home run in 'The House That Ruth Built.' It feels better because we won."

An Exclusive Club

It was 9:25 p.m. on a balmy Friday night at Pacific Bell Park when Barry Bonds made history—again. This time, fireworks were set off from McCovey Cove, the crowd went wild and there was a mob scene at home plate. The huge scoreboard told the story, flashing "600" repeatedly.

On Aug. 9, 2002, Bonds sent a 2-1 pitch from Pittsburgh Pirates right-hander Kip Wells over the center field wall in the sixth inning for his 600th home run, thereby becoming the fourth man in history to do so behind Hank Aaron (755), Babe Ruth (714) and Willie Mays (660).

"Nothing's more satisfying than doing this before about 40,000 friends in San Francisco," a beaming Bonds said. "Nothing could be more gratifying than that. My wife was telling me to hurry up and get it over with. I told her, 'Tonight is it. I'm going to do it today.' She would have had some choice words if I didn't come through."

The Pirates didn't mind the lengthy celebration following the milestone mash. They were ahead at the time and held on for a 4-3 victory. Wells didn't mind having his name etched in the recordbooks and catcher Jason Kendall summed up: "That wasn't a bad pitch, a 96-mph fastball down, and he hit the stuffing out of it—impressive."

One week later, the Giants officially honored the feat by having Aaron and Mays present to pay tribute to the newest member of the 600 Club. Ruth's grandson, Tom Stevens, represented the Babe. Aaron reiterated that Bonds could reach his 755 and Bonds disputed that claim.

"I feel overjoyed and overwhelmed being in the class of these great athletes," an emotional Bonds said. "I'm speechless. This is a night I'll never forget. And to all you little children out there: Dreams really do come true."

Bonds's Burden Lifted

He never received the ring he really wanted in 2002, the one inscribed "World Series Champion," yet Barry Bonds gained personal fulfillment with his remarkable redemption in the postseason. After entering with a paltry .196 average and merely one home run and six RBI in his previous 27 playoff games and 97 at-bats, Bonds erupted with a record eight home runs and a .356 average.

"The dream came true—finally, I made it to this game," Bonds said prior to Game 1 of the World Series, and he promptly homered on his first at-bat. "I don't care about that. I just want to win. It probably took the tension off a little, but games aren't won in the first inning; they're won in the ninth.

"The World Series is what it's about. We got where we wanted to as a team. Unfortunately, we lost the seventh game. Once I got past the tomahawk chop—it haunted me for 10 years—it was a fun time. As a team, we have nothing to be ashamed of. We just have a little more work to do."

Bonds seemed happiest about clearing that troublesome first round. He's never done that before, failing three straight years with the Pittsburgh Pirates (1990-92) and in 1997 and 2000 with the Giants. While with the Bucs, the Atlanta Braves were always the culprit, limiting him to 10 hits in 50 playoff at-bats (.200).

So there was tremendous satisfaction when the Giants edged the Braves 3-2 in the first round, winning the last two games to do it. He batted .294 with three homers against Atlanta pitching, added a .273 average against the St. Louis Cardinals in the NLCS and crowned a brilliant October with a .471 average and four home runs in the World Series.

The Mark of Greatness

"I don't shake my head and say, 'How did he do that?'—he's done it about a hundred thousand times," Dusty Baker said of Barry Bonds. "You do find yourself saying, 'Man, he's done it again.' It's not, 'How did he do it?' It's the fact he keeps doing it, the fact that everybody in the ballpark expects it. But everybody knows Michael Jordan is going to take the last shot of the game... You know Mario Lemieux is going to shoot the puck, have an assist.

"Joe Montana is going to go to Jerry Rice, everybody knows it. Jerry Rice is open some kind of way—touchdown. That's what true greatness is all about, similar to guys like Rickey Henderson— you know he's going to steal."

An Incredible Encore

Nobody thought Barry Bonds could top his 2001 season, yet in some ways 2002 was even better. The voting baseball writers thought so, too—they unanimously made him the National League MVP for a fifth time.

"This year, I kind of ran away with it a little bit," said Bonds, who followed his 73-homer season by winning his first batting title (.370), extending his walks record (198) and shattering Ted Williams' on-base percentage mark with a staggering .582.

"I'm trying to figure out how a 38-year-old is still playing like this. I'm overjoyed, really, especially coming off a 73-homer year to stay consistent. It was a better season than last because we got to the World Series."

It marked the third consecutive year a Giant was honored as MVP, the 10th time overall. Kent was the winner in 2000. Others were Carl Hubbell (1933 and 1936), Willie Mays (1954 and 1965), Willie McCovey (1969) and Kevin Mitchell (1989).

Chasing the Hammer

The only record seemingly left for Barry Bonds following his incredible 2001-2002 seasons is the all-time home run mark of 755 set by Hank Aaron. Bonds, who entered 2003 with 613 homers, doesn't think he'll have enough walkless at-bats to surpass Hammerin' Hank, pointing to younger sluggers like Sammy Sosa and Alex Rodriguez as more likely recordbreakers.

"There's not enough time for me, and that's just reality," said Bonds, who needed to average 47.7 homers over three years (2003-05) to pass Aaron. "You walk me 100-plus times [a year], and that's time I've lost.

"I think A-Rod is the guy you need to watch," he added, referring to Rodriguez, who had 298 home runs entering 2003. "The guy's 27 years old, and I think he's not hit under 40 homers except his first two years in baseball."

Aaron, however, said he felt that Bonds was selling himself short, conceding that the 2001-2002 seasons placed him at a higher level. The Hammer added that he changed his mind after originally tabbing Ken Griffey Jr. as the most likely to reach 756.

"I think Barry can go an awful long way—he's in tremendous shape," Aaron said after Bonds joined the 600 Club in 2002. "He has a great chance to do it if he stays healthy, and I think he will.

"When you reach a certain age, people say you should be going the other direction. Barry has demonstrated to me that he has elevated his game to where he needs to go, and he's even a better ballplayer today than he was five or six years ago."

Bonds reiterated his belief that Aaron's record is attainable, but not by him, when he reported to camp in 2003 and candidly declared: "I think I shot my wad the last two years. I'm not lying—expectations are too high. Hank isn't out of reach. Maybe for me, but he's not out of reach."

What They Say About Barry

"He's a great hitter, a true hitter, a pure hitter. He's a Tony Gwynn, a Wade Boggs, a Roger Maris, a Willie Mays, a Ted Williams and a Mickey Mantle all rolled into one. He's a pretty damn good hitter."
—*Jack Clark*

"Hey, man, he was a hitter before he was hitting the long ball. He's not a slugger—he's a slugger who can hit. Barry can do whatever he wants to do. He's like an upperclassman playing with freshmen and sophomores."
—*Dusty Baker*

"It's hard to imagine any player doing everything better than him—hitting, playing the field. The only thing you could think of is throwing. If you want to say Willie Mays was better at throwing harder, that's probably the case. But other than that, I just don't see it."
—Gary Sheffield

"Barry might be the greatest player who ever played the game. I can't imagine any player being better than he is. I know people talk about Hank Aaron and Willie Mays, but I find it hard to believe anyone has ever been better than Barry."
—Jeff Bagwell

"Best swing I've seen on a left-handed hitter. Ted Williams had a great swing, and Rod Carew. But this kid is so powerful, the ball just goes off his bat. He's just remarkable. If they had pitched to him last year, he mighta hit 90 home runs."
—Ernie Banks in 2002

"I don't think I've seen a hitter in recent memory as locked in the way he is. This guy identifies the pitch almost before the pitcher lets it go. And when he swings at it, he doesn't miss it."
—Bob Brenly in 2001

"He figures out stuff a little quicker than the rest of us. In one at-bat, he'll figure out what a guy throws and exactly what kind of stuff he's got. It might take the rest of us half a year."
—Shawon Dunston

"He's the Muhammad Ali of baseball. The Joe Namath. He talks a lot of stuff, but he backs it up. He's the best player I've ever seen in my life. Barry Bonds might be the greatest player of all time."
—Jim Leyland

"It's Barry, and then everyone else. He's the best player in the game, and there's really nobody close."
—*Eric Karros*

"Nobody else comes close to doing what he does. It's too bad there aren't more all-around players to push him in the National League, but I think Barry is the kind of guy who pushes himself."
—*Orlando Cepeda*

"He's beginning to make a case for himself as arguably being maybe the greatest player to ever play the game."
—*Jim Tracy*

"He's always been the best player in the game. He's always been a complete player. He didn't have to hit 30 extra home runs to convince me of that."
—*Greg Maddux*

"To me, what he did last year was probably the most remarkable thing that's ever happened in the game. To walk 177 times and hit 73 home runs? It was like: The only time he swings, he hits a home run."
—*Tim Raines*

"I can't imagine what it was like seeing Ruth, Williams, Aaron, Mays, DiMaggio and Cobb in the prime of their careers. But somehow, it must have been like what we see Barry doing right now. He completely dominates the game, just as the great stars of their day did."
—*Tom Candiotti in 2002*

"Barry's cocky as hell, but he can back his stuff up. Sometimes you shake your head and wonder how he does what he does. There's nothing this man can't do. I'm a big fan of Barry's, and he know it. But Barry won't let anybody get too close."
—*Tony Gwynn*

"He changed overnight. He's not only a better player, but a better person. Once he got to 500 [homers], he relaxed. A few years before, some guys wouldn't be happy for him. Now, that's changed."

—*Shawon Dunston*

"As a pitcher you look to see if you can fool a hitter. You never fool Barry. You throw a slider that's a half-inch off the plate, and he doesn't even move. It drives you crazy. You start believing that he's totally locked in on you. There's no one area where you can wear him out."

—*Denny Neagle*